German
Picture Dictionary

German
Picture Dictionary

Berlitz Kids™
Berlitz Publishing Company, Inc.

Princeton   Mexico City   Dublin
Eschborn   Singapore

Berlitz Kids is a trademark of, and the Berlitz name and logotype
are registered trademarks of, Berlitz Investment Corporation.

Cover illustration by Chris L. Demarest
Interior illustrations by Chris L. Demarest (pages 3, 5, 7-9, 12-23, 26-43,
46-51, 54-67, 70-75, 78-85, 88-107, and 110-119)
Anna DiVito (pages 24, 25, 52, 53, 76, 77, 86, 87, and 120-123)
Claude Martinot (pages 10, 11, 44, 45, 68, 69, 108, and 109)

Printed in USA

3   5   7   9   10   8   6   4   2

ISBN 2–8315–6255–4

Dear Parents,

The Berlitz Kids™ *Picture Dictionary* will create hours of fun and productive learning for you and your child. Children love sharing books with adults, and reading together is a natural way for your child to develop second-language skills in an enjoyable and entertaining way.

In 1878, Professor Maximilian Berlitz had a revolutionary idea about making language learning accessible and fun. These same principles are still successfully at work today. Now, more than a century later, people all over the world recognize and appreciate his innovative approach. Berlitz Kids™ combines the time-honored traditions of Professor Berlitz with current research to create superior products that truly help children learn foreign languages.

Berlitz Kids™ materials let your child gain access to a second language in a positive way. The content and vocabulary in this book have been carefully chosen by language experts to provide basic words and phrases that form the foundation of a core vocabulary. In addition, the book will delight your child, since each word is used in an amusing sentence in both languages, and then illustrated in an engaging style. The pictures are a great way to capture your child's attention!

You will notice that most words are listed as separate entries. Every so often, though, there is a special page that shows words grouped together by theme. For example, if your child is especially interested in animals, he or she will find a special Animals page with lots of words and pictures grouped there—in both English and the foreign language. In addition, to help your child with phrases used in basic conversation, you and your child may want to look at the back of the book, where phrases about such things as meeting new people and a family dinner can be found.

The Berlitz Kids™ *Picture Dictionary* has an easy-to-use index at the back of the book. This index lists the words in alphabetical order in the second language, and then gives the English translation, and the page number where the word appears in the main part of the book.

We hope the Berlitz Kids™ *Picture Dictionary* will provide you and your child with hours of enjoyable learning.

The Editors at Berlitz Kids™

a/an
ein

A sandwich and an apple are the cat's lunch.

Ein Butterbrot und ein Apfel sind das Mittagessen der Katze.

across
gegenüber

The fork is across from the spoon.

Die Gabel ist gegenüber vom Löffel.

to add
zusammenzählen

I like to add numbers.

Ich zähle Zahlen gern zusammen.

adventure
das Abenteuer

What an adventure!

Was für ein Abenteuer!

afraid, to be
Angst haben

The elephant is afraid.

Der Elefant hat Angst.

after
nach

She eats an apple after lunch.

Nach dem Mittagessen isst sie einen Apfel.

again
wieder

She jumps again and again.

Sie springt immer wieder hoch.

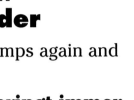

to agree
sich einigen

They need to agree.

Sie sollten sich einigen.

air
die Luft

A balloon is full of air.

Ein Ballon ist voller Luft.

airplane *See Transportation (page 108).*
das Flugzeug *Siehe Transport (Seite 108).*

airport
der Flughafen

Airplanes land at an airport.

Flugzeuge landen auf einem Flughafen.

all
alle

All the frogs are green.

Die Frösche sind alle grün.

alligator *See Animals (page 10).*
der Alligator *Siehe Tiere (Seite 10).*

almost
fast

He can almost reach it.

Er kann es fast erreichen.

along
entlang

There are birds along the path.

Es gibt Vögel entlang des Weges.

already
schon

He already has a hat.

Er hat schon eine Mütze.

and
und

I have two sisters and two brothers.

Ich habe zwei Schwestern und zwei Brüder.

to answer
antworten

Who wants to answer the teacher's question?

Wer will auf die Frage der Lehrerin antworten?

8

ant *See Insects (page 52).*
die Ameise *Siehe Insekten (Seite 52).*

apartment
die Wohnung

He is in the apartment.

**Er ist in der
Wohnung.**

apple
der Apfel

The apple is falling.

**Der Apfel fällt
herunter.**

April
der April

The month after
March is April.

**Der Monat nach dem
März ist der April.**

arm *See People (page 76).*
der Arm *Siehe Menschen (Seite 76).*

armadillo
das Gürteltier

Some armadillos
live in Mexico.

**Einige Gürteltiere
leben in Mexiko.**

around
um

Someone is walking
around the stool.

**Jemand läuft
um den Hocker.**

art
die Kunst

Is it art?

Ist das Kunst?

as
so ... wie

He is as tall
as a tree!

**Er ist so groß wie
ein Baum!**

Animals
Tiere

kangaroo
das Känguru

monkey
der Affe

lion
der Löwe

elephant
der Elefant

bear
der Bär

giraffe
die Giraffe

jaguar
der Jaguar

llama
das Lama

alligator
der Alligator

snake
die Schlange

fox
der Fuchs

hippopotamus
das Nilpferd

cow
die Kuh

horse
das Pferd

rooster
der Hahn

goat
die Ziege

rabbit
das Kaninchen

sheep
das Schaf

chicken
das Huhn

pig
das Schwein

fish
der Fisch

duck
die Ente

frog
der Frosch

11

to ask
fragen

It is time to ask,
"Where are my sheep?"

**Es wird Zeit, dass
du fragst: „Wo sind
meine Schafe?"**

aunt
die Tante

My aunt is my
mom's sister.

**Meine Tante ist
die Schwester
meiner Mutti.**

at
zu

The cat is
at home.

**Die Katze ist
zu Hause.**

awake
wach

The duck is awake.

Die Ente ist wach.

attic *See Rooms in a House (page 86).*
der Dachboden *Siehe Räume in einem
Haus (Seite 86).*

away
weg

The cat is
going away.

**Die Katze
fährt weg.**

August
der August

The month after
July is August.

**Der Monat nach
dem Juli ist
der August.**

baby
das Baby

The baby likes
to eat bananas.

**Das Baby isst
gern Bananen.**

ball
der Ball

Can he catch
the ball?

**Kann er den
Ball fangen?**

back
der Rücken

She is scratching
his back.

**Sie kratzt ihm
den Rücken.**

balloon
der Ballon

It is a balloon!

Das ist ein Ballon!

bad
schlimm

What a bad,
bad monster!

**Was für ein
schlimmes,
schlimmes Monster!**

banana
die Banane

The bananas
are in the bowl.

**Die Bananen sind
in der Schüssel.**

bag
die Tüte

The bag is full.

Die Tüte ist voll.

band
die Kapelle

The band is loud.

Die Kapelle ist laut.

bakery
die Bäckerei

Mmm! Everything at
the bakery smells great!

**Mmm! Alles in der
Bäckerei riecht
großartig!**

bandage
das Pflaster

She has a bandage
on her knee.

**Sie hat ein Pflaster
auf dem Knie.**

bank
das Sparschwein

Put your money into the bank!

Steck dein Geld ins Sparschwein!

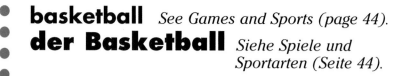

barber
der Friseur

The barber cuts my hair.

Der Friseur schneidet mir die Haare.

to bark
bellen

Dogs like to bark.

Hunde bellen gern.

baseball *See Games and Sports (page 44).*
der Baseball *Siehe Spiele und Sportarten (Seite 44).*

basement *See Rooms in a House (page 86).*
der Keller *Siehe Räume in einem Haus (Seite 86).*

basket
der Korb

What is in the basket?

Was ist im Korb?

basketball *See Games and Sports (page 44).*
der Basketball *Siehe Spiele und Sportarten (Seite 44).*

bat
die Fledermaus

The bat is sleeping.

Die Fledermaus schläft.

bat
der Schläger

Hit the ball with the bat!

Schlag den Ball mit dem Schläger!

bath
das Bad

She is taking a bath.

Sie nimmt ein Bad.

bathroom *See Rooms in a House (page 86).*
das Badezimmer *Siehe Räume in einem Haus (Seite 86).*

to be
sein

Would you like to be my friend?

Möchtest du mein Freund sein?

beach
der Strand

I like to play
at the beach.

**Ich spiele gern
am Strand.**

beans
die Bohnen

He likes to eat beans.

**Er isst gern
Bohnen.**

bear   *See Animals (page 10).*
der Bär   *Siehe Tiere (Seite 10).*

beautiful
schön

Look at the
beautiful things.

**Schau dir die
schönen Dinge an.**

because
weil

She is wet
because it is raining.

**Sie ist nass,
weil es regnet.**

bed
das Bett

The bed is next
to the table.

**Das Bett ist neben
dem Tisch.**

bedroom   *See Rooms in a House (page 86).*
das Schlafzimmer   *Siehe Räume in
einem Haus (Seite 86).*

bee   *See Insects (page 52).*
die Biene   *Siehe Insekten (Seite 52).*

beetle   *See Insects (page 52).*
der Käfer   *Siehe Insekten (Seite 52).*

before
bevor

Put on your socks
before you put on
your shoes.

**Zieh dir die Socken
an, bevor du dir die
Schuhe anziehst.**

to begin
anfangen

She wants to begin
the painting.

**Sie möchte mit dem
Malen anfangen.**

behind
hinter

The boy is
behind the tree.

**Der Junge
ist hinter
dem Baum.**

to believe
glauben

This is too
good to believe.

**Das ist doch
kaum zu glauben.**

bell
die Glocke

Don't ring that bell!

**Läute die Glocke
nicht!**

belt *See Clothing (page 24).*
der Gürtel *Siehe Kleidung (Seite 24).*

berry
die Beere

Those berries
look good.

**Diese Beeren da
sehen gut aus.**

best
am besten

The red box
is the best.

**Die rote Schachtel
ist am besten.**

better
besser

The belt is better
than the pin.

**Der Gürtel ist
besser als die Nadel.**

between
zwischen

He is between
two trees.

**Er ist zwischen
zwei Bäumen.**

bicycle *See Transportation (page 108).*
das Fahrrad *Siehe Transport (Seite 108).*

big
groß

He is very big.

Er ist sehr groß.

biking *See Games and Sports (page 44).*
das Radfahren *Siehe Spiele und Sportarten (Seite 44).*

bird
der Vogel

The bird is flying south for winter.

Der Vogel fliegt für den Winter nach Süden.

birthday
der Geburtstag

She is one year old today. Happy birthday!

Sie wird heute ein Jahr alt. Alles Gute zum Geburtstag!

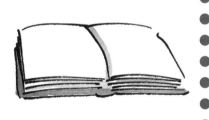

black *See Numbers and Colors (page 68).*
schwarz *Siehe Zahlen und Farben (Seite 68).*

blank
unbeschrieben

The pages are blank.

Die Seiten sind unbeschrieben.

blanket
die Decke

What is under that blue blanket?

Was ist unter der blauen Decke?

blouse *See Clothing (page 24).*
die Bluse *Siehe Kleidung (Seite 24).*

to blow
blasen

The wind is starting to blow.

Der Wind beginnt zu blasen.

blue *See Numbers and Colors (page 68).*
blau *Siehe Zahlen und Farben (Seite 68).*

boat *See Transportation (page 108).*
das Boot *Siehe Transport (Seite 108).*

book
das Buch

I am reading a book.

Ich lese ein Buch.

bookstore
die Buchhandlung

You can buy a book at a bookstore.

Man kann ein Buch in einer Buchhandlung kaufen.

boots *See Clothing (page 24).*
die Stiefel *Siehe Kleidung (Seite 24).*

bottle
die Flasche

The straw is in
the bottle.

**Der Strohhalm ist
in der Flasche.**

bowl
die Schale

Some food is still
in the bowl.

**Es ist noch
etwas Essen
in der Schale.**

bowling *See Games and Sports (page 44).*
das Kegeln *Siehe Spiele und Sportarten
(Seite 44).*

box
die Kiste

Why is that fox
in the box?

**Warum ist dieser
Fuchs da in
der Kiste?**

boy
der Junge

The boys
are brothers.

**Die Jungen sind
Brüder.**

branch
der Ast

Oh, no! Get off
that tree branch!

**O nein! Geh von
dem Ast da runter!**

brave
mutig

What a brave
mouse!

**Was für eine
mutige Maus!**

bread
das Brot

He likes bread with
jam and butter.

**Er mag Brot mit
Marmelade
und Butter.**

to break
zerbrechen

It is easy to
break an egg.

**Es ist einfach, ein
Ei zu zerbrechen.**

breakfast
das Frühstück

Morning is the time
for breakfast.

**Der Morgen ist
die Zeit für das
Frühstück.**

bridge
die Brücke

The boat is under the bridge.

Das Boot ist unter der Brücke.

to bring
bringen

She wants to bring the lamb to school.

Sie will das Lamm zur Schule bringen.

broom
der Besen

A broom is for sweeping.

Ein Besen ist zum Kehren.

brother
der Bruder

He is my brother.

Er ist mein Bruder.

brown *See Numbers and Colors (page 68).*
braun *Siehe Zahlen und Farben (Seite 68).*

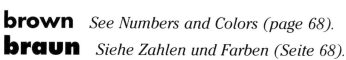

brush
die Bürste

I need my hairbrush.

Ich brauche meine Haarbürste.

bubble
die Seifenblase

The bathtub is full of bubbles.

Die Badewanne ist voll von Seifenblasen.

bug
der Käfer

Do you know the name of this bug?

Weißt du, wie dieser Käfer heißt?

to build
bauen

I want to build a box.

Ich will eine Kiste bauen.

bump
der Hubbel

The bicycle hit a bump.

Das Rad ist über einen Hubbel gefahren.

bus *See Transportation (page 108).*
der Bus *Siehe Transport (Seite 108).*

butterfly *See Insects (page 52).*
der Schmetterling *Siehe Insekten (Seite 52).*

bush
der Busch

A bird is in the bush.

Ein Vogel ist im Busch.

button
der Knopf

One button is missing.

Ein Knopf fehlt.

busy
beschäftigt

He is very busy.

Er ist sehr beschäftigt.

to buy
kaufen

He wants to buy a banana.

Er will eine Banane kaufen.

but
aber

The pencil is on the table, but the book is on the chair.

Der Bleistift ist auf dem Tisch, aber das Buch ist auf dem Stuhl.

by
bei

She is standing by the cheese.

Sie steht bei dem Käse.

butter
die Butter

The bread and butter taste good.

Das Brot und die Butter schmecken gut.

cage
der Käfig

The bird is
on the cage.

**Der Vogel ist
auf dem Käfig.**

camera
die Kamera

Smile at the
camera!

**Lächle in die
Kamera!**

cake
der Kuchen

She likes to
eat cake.

**Sie isst gern
Kuchen.**

can
die Dose

What is in
that can?

**Was ist in
der Dose?**

to call
anrufen
(...zu...)

Remember to call
me again later.

**Denk daran, mich
später wieder
anzurufen.**

candle
die Kerze

She is lighting
the candle.

**Sie zündet die
Kerze an.**

camel
das Kamel

The camel is hot.

**Dem Kamel
ist heiß.**

candy
der Bonbon

Candy is sweet.

Bonbons sind süß.

cap *See Clothing (page 24).*
die Mütze *Siehe Kleidung (Seite 24).*

car *See Transportation (page 108).*
das Auto *Siehe Transport (Seite 108).*

card
die Karte

Do you want
to play cards?

**Willst du Karten
spielen?**

to carry
tragen

Are you sure you
want to carry that?

**Bist du sicher,
dass du das
tragen willst?**

to care
versorgen

Her job is to
care for pets.

**Ihre Aufgabe ist es,
Tiere zu versorgen.**

castanets
die Kastagnetten

Click the castanets
to the music!

**Klick mit den
Kastagnetten
zur Musik!**

carpenter
der Zimmermann

A carpenter makes
things with wood.

**Ein Zimmermann
macht Sachen
aus Holz.**

castle
das Schloss

The king lives
in a castle.

**Der König lebt in
einem Schloss.**

carrot
die Karotte

A carrot is orange.

**Eine Karotte
ist orange.**

cat
die Katze

The cat sees
the mouse.

**Die Katze sieht
die Maus.**

caterpillar *See Insects (page 52).*
die Raupe *Siehe Insekten (Seite 52).*

to catch
fangen

He runs to catch the ball.

Er läuft, um den Ball zu fangen.

cave
die Höhle

Who lives in the cave?

Wer lebt in der Höhle?

to celebrate
feiern

They are here to celebrate his birthday.

Sie sind da, um seinen Geburtstag zu feiern.

chair
der Stuhl

He is sitting on a chair.

Er sitzt auf einem Stuhl.

chalk
die Kreide

You can write with chalk.

Man kann mit Kreide schreiben.

to change
wechseln

He wants to change his shirt.

Er will sein Hemd wechseln.

to cheer
zujubeln (...zu...)

It is fun to cheer for our team.

Es macht Spaß, unserer Mannschaft zuzujubeln.

cheese
der Käse

The mouse likes to eat cheese.

Die Maus frisst gern Käse.

Clothing
Kleidung

vest
die Weste

hat
der Hut

raincoat
der Regenmantel

cap
die Mütze

earmuffs
die Ohrenschützer

jacket
die Jacke

shirt
das Hemd

tie
die Krawatte

belt
der Gürtel

pants
die Hosen

gloves
die Handschuhe

socks
die Socken

sneakers
die Turnschuhe

dress
das Kleid

coat
der Mantel

mittens
die Fäustlinge

boots
die Stiefel

scarf
der Schal

blouse
die Bluse

sweater
die Strickjacke

skirt
der Rock

shoes
die Schuhe

shawl
das Umhängetuch

25

cherry
die Kirsche

He wants a cherry.

Er will eine Kirsche.

circus
der Zirkus

There are clowns
at a circus.

**In einem Zirkus
gibt es Clowns.**

chicken *See Animals (page 10).*
das Huhn *Siehe Tiere (Seite 10).*

child
das Kind

She is a
happy child.

**Sie ist ein
fröhliches Kind.**

city
die Stadt

This cow does not
live in the city.

**Diese Kuh wohnt
nicht in der Stadt.**

chocolate
die Schokolade

He likes chocolate.

Er mag Schokolade.

to clap
klatschen

He likes to clap
when he is happy.

**Er klatscht gern,
wenn er sich freut.**

circle
der Kreis

It is drawing
a circle.

**Er zeichnet
einen Kreis.**

class
die Klasse

There is an elephant
in my class.

**In meiner Klasse
ist ein Elefant.**

classroom
das Klassenzimmer

A teacher works in a classroom.

Ein Lehrer arbeitet in einem Klassenzimmer.

clean
sauber

The car is very clean.

Das Auto ist ganz sauber.

to clean
putzen

He is starting to clean his room.

Er beginnt, sein Zimmer zu putzen.

to climb
klettern

The bear likes to climb the tree.

Der Bär klettert gern auf den Baum.

clock
die Uhr

A clock tells time.

Eine Uhr zeigt die Zeit an.

close
nahe

The turtle is close to the rock.

Die Schildkröte ist nahe beim Stein.

to close
schließen

He is going to close the window.

Er wird das Fenster schließen.

closet *See Rooms in a House (page 86).*
der Schrank *Siehe Räume in einem Haus (Seite 86).*

cloud
die Wolke

The sun is behind the cloud.

Die Sonne ist hinter der Wolke.

clown
der Clown

The clown
is funny.

**Der Clown
ist lustig.**

coat *See Clothing (page 24).*
der Mantel *Siehe Kleidung (Seite 24).*

cold
kalt

It is cold
in here!

**Es ist kalt hier
drinnen!**

comb
der Kamm

Where is
my comb?

**Wo ist mein
Kamm?**

to comb
kämmen

He likes to comb
his hair.

**Er kämmt sich
gern die Haare.**

to come
kommen

He wants them to
come over here.

**Er möchte, dass sie
herüberkommen.**

computer
der Computer

I think she is working
at her computer too long.

**Ich glaube, sie
arbeitet schon zu
lange an ihrem
Computer.**

to cook
kochen

It is fun to cook.

**Das Kochen
macht Spaß.**

cookie
das Plätzchen

Mary wants
a cookie.

**Maria möchte ein
Plätzchen.**

to count
zählen

There are too many
stars to count.

**Es gibt zu viele Sterne,
um sie zu zählen.**

country
die Landschaft

The country
is beautiful.

**Die Landschaft
ist schön.**

cow *See Animals (page 10).*
die Kuh *Siehe Tiere (Seite 10).*

crayon
der Buntstift

She is drawing
with her crayons.

**Sie zeichnet mit
ihren Buntstiften.**

cricket *See Games and Sports (page 44).*
das Kricket *Siehe Spiele und Sportarten
(Seite 44).*

cricket *See Insects (page 52).*
die Grille *Siehe Insekten (Seite 52).*

crowded
überfüllt

This elevator
is crowded.

**Dieser Aufzug
ist überfüllt.**

to cry
weinen

Try not to cry!

**Versucht, nicht
zu weinen!**

cup
die Tasse

He is drinking water
from the cup.

**Er trinkt Wasser
aus der Tasse.**

to cut
schneiden

Use a knife to cut
the carrots!

**Nimm ein Messer,
um die Karotten
zu schneiden!**

cute
niedlich

She thinks her
baby is cute.

**Sie findet ihr
Baby niedlich.**

dad
Vati

My dad and
I look alike.

**Mein Vati und ich
sehen uns ähnlich.**

**to dance
tanzen**

The pig likes to dance
and play the drum.

**Das Schwein tanzt
und trommelt gern.**

**danger
die Gefahr**

He is in danger.

Er ist in Gefahr.

**dark
dunkel**

It is dark at night.

**Nachts ist
es dunkel.**

**day
der Tag**

The sun shines in the day.

**Die Sonne scheint
am Tag.**

**December
der Dezember**

The month after
November is December.

**Der Monat nach
dem November ist
der Dezember.**

**to decide
sich entscheiden**

It is hard to decide.

**Es ist schwer, sich
zu entscheiden.**

**decision
die Entscheidung**

That is a good
decision.

**Das ist eine gute
Entscheidung.**

deck   *See Rooms in a House (page 86).*
die Holzterrasse   *Siehe Räume in einem
Haus (Seite 86).*

**decorations
die Dekorationen**

The decorations
look great!

**Die Dekorationen
sehen toll aus!**

deer
das Reh

The deer is running in the woods.

Das Reh läuft im Wald.

dentist
die Zahnärztin

The dentist has a big job.

Die Zahnärztin hat viel Arbeit.

department
die Abteilung (...abteilung)

This is the hat department.

Das ist die Hutabteilung.

desk
der Schreibtisch

The desk is very messy.

Der Schreibtisch ist sehr unordentlich.

different
anders

The one in the middle is different.

Der in der Mitte ist anders.

difficult
schwer

This is difficult!

Das ist schwer!

to dig
graben

A dog uses its paws to dig.

Ein Hund benutzt seine Pfoten, um zu graben.

dining room
das Esszimmer

See Rooms in a House (page 86).

Siehe Räume in einem Haus (Seite 86).

dinner
das Abendessen

We have dinner at 6 o'clock.

Um 6 Uhr ist das Abendessen fertig.

dinosaur
der Dinosaurier

The dinosaur is having fun.

Der Dinosaurier hat Spaß.

dirty
schmutzig

The pig is dirty.

Das Schwein ist schmutzig.

doll
die Puppe

The doll is in a box.

Die Puppe ist in einer Schachtel.

dish
das Geschirr

Do not drop the dishes!

Lass das Geschirr nicht fallen!

dolphin
der Delphin

Dolphins live in the sea.

Delphine leben im Meer.

to do
tun

He has a lot to do.

Er hat viel zu tun.

donkey
der Esel

The donkey is sleeping.

Der Esel schläft.

doctor
der Arzt

The doctor checks the baby.

Der Arzt untersucht das Baby.

door
die Tür

What is behind the door?

Was ist hinter der Tür?

dog
der Hund

The dog has a funny hat.

Der Hund hat einen lustigen Hut.

down
unten

The elevator is going down.

Der Aufzug fährt nach unten.

dragon
der Drache

The dragon is
cooking lunch.

**Der Drache kocht
das Mittagessen.**

to draw
zeichnen

He likes to draw.

Er zeichnet gern.

drawing
die Zeichnung

Look at my drawing!

**Schau dir meine
Zeichnung an!**

dress *See Clothing (page 24).*
das Kleid *Siehe Kleidung (Seite 24).*

to drink
trinken

She likes to drink milk.

Sie trinkt gern Milch.

to drive
fahren

He is too small
to drive.

**Er ist zu klein, um
selbst zu fahren.**

to drop
fallen lassen

He is going to
drop the pie.

**Er wird den Kuchen
fallen lassen.**

drum
die Trommel

He can play
the drum.

**Er kann Trommel
spielen.**

dry
trocken

The shirt is dry.

**Das Hemd ist
trocken.**

duck *See Animals (page 10).*
die Ente *Siehe Tiere (Seite 10).*

dust
der Staub

There is dust
under the bed.

**Unter dem Bett
ist Staub.**

E

each
jede

Each snowflake
is different.

**Jede Schneeflocke
ist anders.**

ear *See People (page 76).*
das Ohr *Siehe Menschen (Seite 76).*

early
früh

The sun comes up
early in the day.

**Die Sonne geht früh
am Tag auf.**

earmuffs *See Clothing (page 24).*
die Ohrenschützer *Siehe Kleidung (Seite 24).*

to earn
verdienen

We work to earn money.

**Wir arbeiten, um
Geld zu verdienen.**

east
der Osten

The sun comes
up in the east.

**Die Sonne geht
im Osten auf.**

to eat
(fr)essen

This bird likes
to eat worms.

**Dieser Vogel (fr)isst
gern Würmer.**

egg
das Ei

The hen has laid
an egg.

**Die Henne hat
ein Ei gelegt.**

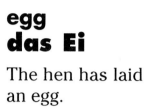

eight *See Numbers and Colors (page 68).*
acht *Siehe Zahlen und Farben (Seite 68).*

eighteen *See Numbers and Colors (page 68).*
achtzehn *Siehe Zahlen und Farben (Seite 68).*

eighty *See Numbers and Colors (page 68).*
achtzig *Siehe Zahlen und Farben (Seite 68).*

elephant *See Animals (page 10).*
der Elefant *Siehe Tiere (Seite 10).*

eleven *See Numbers and Colors (page 68).*
elf *Siehe Zahlen und Farben (Seite 68).*

empty
leer

The bottle is empty.

Die Flasche ist leer.

to end
beenden

It is time to end the game.

Es wird Zeit, das Spiel zu beenden.

enough
genug

He has enough food!

Er hat genug Essen!

every
jedes

Every egg is broken.

Jedes Ei ist zerbrochen.

everyone
jeder

Everyone here has spots!

Jeder hier hat Flecken!

everything
alles

Everything is purple.

Alles ist lila.

everywhere
überall

There are balls everywhere.

Überall sind Bälle.

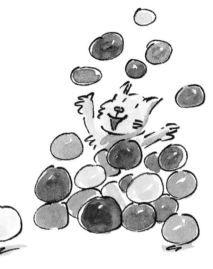

excited
begeistert

He is excited.

Er ist begeistert.

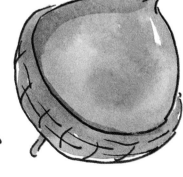

eye *See People (page 76).*
das Auge *Siehe Menschen (Seite 76).*

F

face *See People (page 76).*
das Gesicht *Siehe Menschen (Seite 76).*

factory
die Fabrik

Cans are made in
this factory.

**In dieser Fabrik
werden Dosen
hergestellt.**

to fall
hinfallen

He is about
to fall.

**Er wird gleich
hinfallen.**

fall
der Herbst

It is fall.

Es ist Herbst.

family
die Familie

This is a big
family.

**Dies ist eine
große Familie.**

fan
der Ventilator

Please, turn off
the fan!

**Bitte stell den
Ventilator ab!**

far
weit

The moon is
far away.

**Der Mond ist
weit weg.**

faraway
weit entfernt

She is going to a
faraway place.

**Sie reist an einen
weit entfernten Ort.**

fast
schnell

That train is
going fast!

**Dieser Zug da
fährt schnell!**

fat
dick

The pig
is fat.

**Das Schwein
ist dick.**

father
der Vater

My father and
I look alike.

**Mein Vater und ich
sehen uns ähnlich.**

favorite
liebstes

This is my
favorite toy.

**Das ist mein liebstes
Spielzeug.**

feather
die Feder

The feather is
tickling her nose.

**Die Feder kitzelt
sie an der Nase.**

February
der Februar

The month after
January is February.

**Der Monat nach
dem Januar ist
der Februar.**

to feel
fühlen

He likes to
feel safe.

**Er fühlt sich
gern sicher.**

fence
der Zaun

A zebra is
on my fence.

**Auf meinem Zaun
ist ein Zebra.**

fifteen   *See Numbers and Colors (page 68).*
fünfzehn   *Siehe Zahlen und Farben (Seite 68).*

fifty   *See Numbers and Colors (page 68).*
fünfzig   *Siehe Zahlen und Farben (Seite 68).*

to find
finden

He is trying to
find his kite.

**Er versucht, seinen
Drachen zu finden.**

finger   *See People (page 76).*
der Finger   *Siehe Menschen (Seite 76).*

fire
das Feuer

He can put
out the fire.

**Er kann das
Feuer löschen.**

firefighter
der Feuerwehrmann

The firefighter has boots and a hat.

Der Feuerwehrmann hat Stiefel und einen Hut.

firefly *See Insects (page 52).*
das Glühwürmchen *Siehe Insekten (Seite 52).*

firehouse
das Feuerwehrgebäude

Welcome to the firehouse!

Willkommen im Feuerwehrgebäude!

first
zuerst

The yellow one is first in line.

Das Gelbe steht zuerst in der Schlange.

fish *See Animals (page 10).*
der Fisch *Siehe Tiere (Seite 10).*

five *See Numbers and Colors (page 68).*
fünf *Siehe Zahlen und Farben (Seite 68).*

to fix
reparieren

She wants to fix it.

Sie will es reparieren.

flag
die Fahne

A flag is above her hat.

Über ihrem Hut ist eine Fahne.

flat
platt

The tire is flat.

Der Reifen ist platt.

flea *See Insects (page 52).*
der Floh *Siehe Insekten (Seite 52).*

floor
der Fußboden

There is a hole in the floor.

Im Fußboden ist ein Loch.

flower
die Blume

The flower is
growing.

Die Blume wächst.

flute
die Flöte

Robert plays
the flute.

Robert spielt Flöte.

fly *See Insects (page 52).*
die Fliege *Siehe Insekten (Seite 52).*

to fly
fliegen

The bee wants
to fly.

**Die Biene möchte
fliegen.**

fog
der Nebel

He is walking
in the fog.

**Er geht im Nebel
spazieren.**

food
das Essen

He eats a lot
of food.

**Er isst eine Menge
Essen.**

foot *See People (page 76).*
der Fuß *Siehe Menschen (Seite 76).*

for
für

This is for you.

Dies ist für dich.

to forget
vergessen

He does not want to
forget his lunch!

**Er möchte sein
Mittagessen nicht
vergessen!**

fork
die Gabel

He eats with
a fork.

**Er (fr)isst mit
einer Gabel.**

forty *See Numbers and Colors (page 68).*
vierzig *Siehe Zahlen und Farben (Seite 68).*

four *See Numbers and Colors (page 68).*
vier *Siehe Zahlen und Farben (Seite 68).*

fourteen *See Numbers and Colors (page 68).*
vierzehn *Siehe Zahlen und Farben (Seite 68).*

fox *See Animals (page 10).*
der Fuchs *Siehe Tiere (Seite 10).*

Friday
der Freitag

On Friday, we go
to the park.

**Am Freitag gehen
wir zum Park.**

friend
der Freund

We are good
friends.

**Wir sind gute
Freunde.**

frog *See Animals (page 10).*
der Frosch *Siehe Tiere (Seite 10).*

front
vor

She sits in front
of him.

Sie sitzt vor ihm.

fruit
das Obst

Fruit is
delicious.

Obst ist lecker.

full
voll

The cart is
full of lizards.

**Der Wagen ist voll
von Eidechsen.**

fun
der Spaß

She is having fun.

Sie hat Spaß.

funny
komisch

What a funny face!

**Was für ein
komisches Gesicht!**

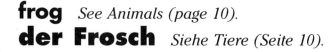

game
das Spiel

We play the game
in the park.

**Wir spielen das
Spiel im Park.**

garage
See Rooms in a House (page 86).
die Garage
*Siehe Räume in einem Haus
(Seite 86).*

garden
der Garten

Roses are growing
in the garden.

**In dem Garten
wachsen Rosen.**

gate
das Tor

The gate is open.

Das Tor ist offen.

to get
bekommen

The mice are trying
to get the cheese.

**Die Mäuse
versuchen, den Käse
zu bekommen.**

giraffe
See Animals (page 10).
die Giraffe
Siehe Tiere (Seite 10).

girl
das Mädchen

The girl is dancing.

Das Mädchen tanzt.

to give
geben

I want to give
you a present.

**Ich möchte dir ein
Geschenk geben.**

glad, to be
sich freuen

She is glad
to see you.

**Sie freut sich,
dich zu sehen.**

glass
das Glas

Windows are made of glass.

Fenster sind aus Glas.

glasses
die Brille

This owl wears glasses.

Diese Eule trägt eine Brille.

gloves *See Clothing (page 24).*
die Handschuhe *Siehe Kleidung (Seite 24).*

to go
gehen

It is time to go to your room.

Es wird Zeit, dass du auf dein Zimmer gehst.

goat *See Animals (page 10).*
die Ziege *Siehe Tiere (Seite 10).*

golf *See Games and Sports (page 44).*
das Golf *Siehe Spiele und Sportarten (Seite 44).*

good
gut

What a good dog!

Was für ein guter Hund!

good-bye
Auf Wiedersehen

Good-bye!

Auf Wiedersehen!

goose
die Gans

A goose is riding a bicycle.

Eine Gans fährt Rad.

gorilla
der Gorilla

The gorilla is
eating a banana.

**Der Gorilla frisst
eine Banane.**

to grab
greifen

She wants to grab
the bananas.

**Sie will nach den
Bananen greifen.**

grandfather
der Großvater

I have fun with
my grandfather.

**Ich habe viel
Spaß mit meinem
Großvater.**

grandma
die Großmutter

Grandma is my
dad's mother.

**Großmutter ist die
Mutter meines Vaters.**

grandmother
die Großmutter

My grandmother
likes to bake.

**Meine Großmutter
bäckt gern.**

grandpa
der Großvater

Grandpa is my
mom's father.

**Großvater ist der
Vater meiner
Mutter.**

grape
die Traube

Get the grapes!

Hol dir die Trauben!

grass
das Gras

Cows eat grass.

Kühe fressen Gras.

grasshopper
die Heuschrecke

See Insects (page 52).

*Siehe Insekten
(Seite 52).*

43

Spiele und Sportarten

baseball
der Baseball

basketball
der Basketball

golf
das Golf

ping-pong
das Tischtennis

running
das Laufen

bowling
das Kegeln

ice skating
das Schlittschuhlaufen

soccer
der Fußball

skiing
das Skilaufen

tennis
das Tennis

biking
das Radfahren

swimming
das Schwimmen

gray *See Numbers and Colors (page 68).*
grau *Siehe Zahlen und Farben (Seite 68).*

great
toll

It is a great party.

**Das ist eine
tolle Party.**

green *See Numbers and Colors (page 68).*
grün *Siehe Zahlen und Farben (Seite 68).*

groceries
die Lebensmittel

The groceries are
falling out.

**Die Lebensmittel
fallen heraus.**

ground
die Erde

They live in
the ground.

**Sie wohnen in
der Erde.**

group
die Gruppe

This is a group
of artists.

**Dies ist eine Gruppe
von Künstlern.**

to grow
wachsen

He wants to grow.

Er möchte wachsen.

to guess
raten

It is fun to guess
what is inside.

**Es macht Spaß zu
raten, was darin ist.**

guitar
die Gitarre

My robot plays
the guitar.

**Mein Roboter
spielt Gitarre.**

hair *See People (page 76).*
das Haar *Siehe Menschen (Seite 76).*

half
halb

Half the cookie is gone.

Das halbe Plätzchen ist verschwunden.

hall *See Rooms in a House (page 86).*
der Flur *Siehe Räume in einem Haus (Seite 86).*

hammer
der Hammer

Hit the nail with the hammer!

Schlagt mit dem Hammer auf den Nagel!

hammock
die Hängematte

Dad is sleeping in the hammock.

Vati schläft in der Hängematte.

hand *See People (page 76).*
Hand *Siehe Menschen (Seite 76).*

happy
fröhlich

This is a happy face.

Dies ist ein fröhliches Gesicht.

hard
hart

The rock is hard.

Der Felsen ist hart.

harp
die Harfe

She plays the harp very well.

Sie spielt sehr gut Harfe.

hat *See Clothing (page 24).*
der Hut *Siehe Kleidung (Seite 24).*

to have
haben

She needs to have three hats.

Sie muss drei Hüte haben.

he
er

He is under the table.

Er ist unter dem Tisch.

head *See People (page 76).*
der Kopf *Siehe Menschen (Seite 76).*

to hear *See People (page 76).*
hören *Siehe Menschen (Seite 76).*

heart
das Herz

The heart is red.

Das Herz ist rot.

helicopter *See Transportation (page 108).*
der Hubschrauber *Siehe Transport (Seite 108).*

hello
Guten Tag

Hello.
How are you?

Guten Tag!
Wie geht es Ihnen?

help
die Hilfe

I need help!

Ich brauche Hilfe!

her
ihr

This is her tail.

Dies ist ihr
Schwanz.

here
hier

I live here.

Ich wohne hier.

hi
hallo

Hi!

Hallo!

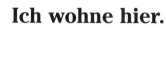

to hide
sich verstecken

She is too big to hide
under the box.

Sie ist zu groß, um
sich unter der Kiste
zu verstecken.

high
hoch

The star is high
in the sky.

Der Stern ist hoch
oben am Himmel.

hill
der Hügel

She is coming
down the hill.

Sie kommt den
Hügel herunter.

hippopotamus *See Animals (page 10).*
das Nilpferd *Siehe Tiere (Seite 10).*

to hit
schlagen

He tries to hit
the ball.

**Er versucht, den
Ball zu schlagen.**

to hold
halten

He has to hold her
hand now.

**Er muss jetzt ihre
Hand halten.**

hole
das Loch

He is digging a hole.

Er gräbt ein Loch.

home
zu Hause

She is at home,
relaxing.

**Sie ist zu Hause und
entspannt sich.**

hooray
hurra

We are winning! Hooray!

Wir gewinnen! Hurra!

to hop
hüpfen

They know how to hop.

**Sie wissen,
wie man hüpft.**

horn
das Horn

He plays the horn.

Er spielt Horn.

horse *See Animals (page 10).*
das Pferd *Siehe Tiere (Seite 10).*

hospital
**das
Krankenhaus**

Doctors work at
the hospital.

**Im Krankenhaus
arbeiten Ärzte.**

hot
heiß

Fire is hot.

Feuer ist heiß.

hotel
das Hotel

He is staying at
the hotel.

**Er übernachtet
im Hotel.**

hour
die Stunde

In an hour, it is going to be two o'clock.

In einer Stunde ist es zwei Uhr.

house
das Haus

The house has many windows.

Das Haus hat viele Fenster.

how
wie

How does he do that?

Wie macht er das denn?

hug
umarmen

Give me a hug!

Umarm mich mal!

huge
riesig

That cat is huge!

Diese Katze ist riesig!

hundred
hundert

See Numbers and Colors (page 68).

Siehe Zahlen und Farben (Seite 68).

hungry
hungrig

I think he is hungry.

Ich glaube, er ist hungrig.

to hurry
sich beeilen

She has to hurry.

Sie muss sich beeilen.

to hurt
wehtun

It does not have to hurt.

Es muss nicht wehtun.

husband
der Ehemann

He is her husband.

Er ist ihr Ehemann.

I
ich

"I am so cute!" she says.

„Ich bin ja so niedlich!", sagt sie.

ice
das Eis

We skate on ice.

Wir laufen auf dem Eis Schlittschuh.

ice cream
die Eiscreme

Clara likes ice cream.

Klara mag Eiscreme.

idea
die Idee

She has an idea.

Sie hat eine Idee.

important
wichtig

He looks very important.

Er sieht sehr wichtig aus.

in
in

What is in that box?

Was ist in der Kiste?

inside
drinnen

He is inside the house.

Er ist im Haus drinnen.

into
in

Do not go into that cave!

Geh ja nicht in diese Höhle!

island
die Insel

The goat is on an island.

Die Ziege ist auf einer Insel.

Insects
Insekten

butterfly
der Schmetterling

wasp
die Wespe

mantis
die Gottesanbeterin

fly
die Fliege

flea
der Floh

beetle
der Käfer

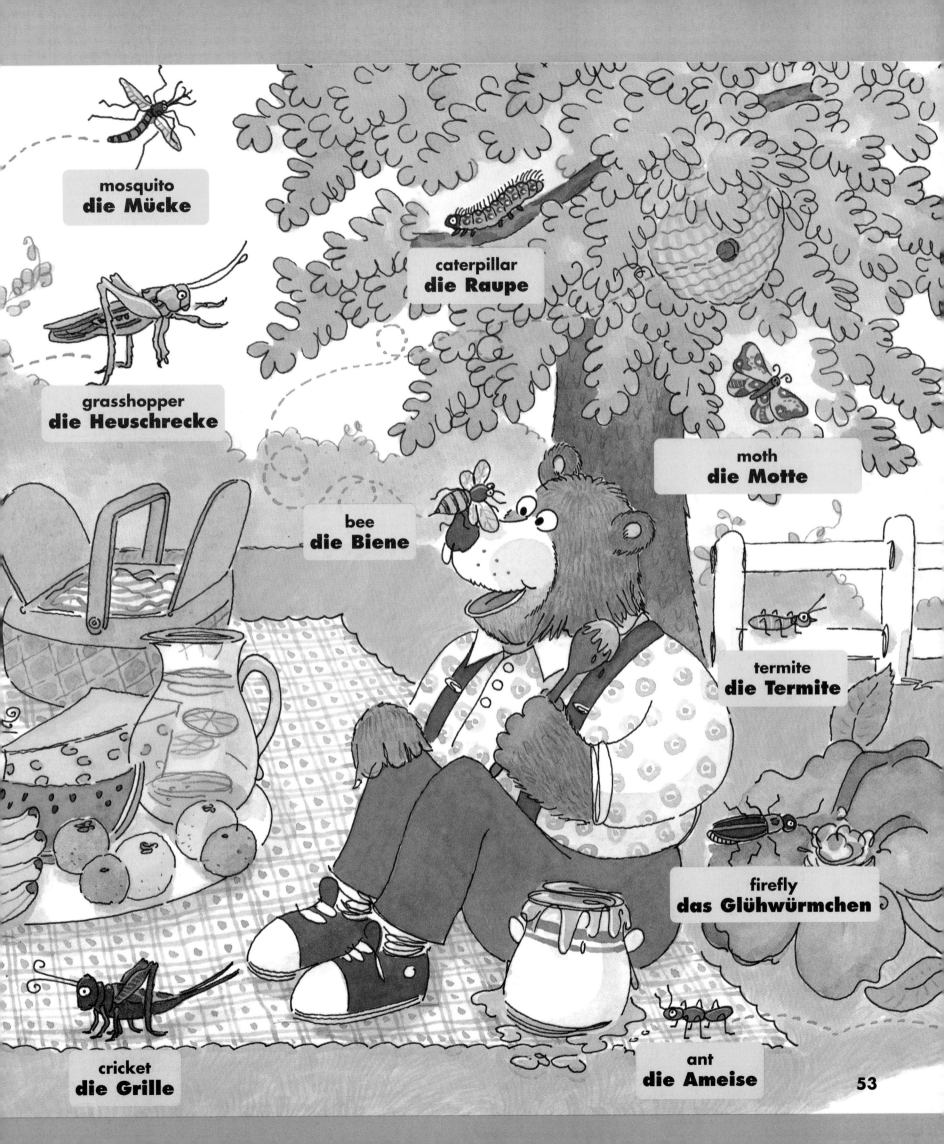

mosquito
die Mücke

caterpillar
die Raupe

grasshopper
die Heuschrecke

moth
die Motte

bee
die Biene

termite
die Termite

firefly
das Glühwürmchen

cricket
die Grille

ant
die Ameise

53

J

jacket *See Clothing (page 24).*
die Jacke *Siehe Kleidung (Seite 24).*

jaguar *See Animals (page 10).*
der Jaguar *Siehe Tiere (Seite 10).*

jam
die Marmelade

Do you think she likes
bread and jam?

**Meinst du, sie mag
Brot mit Marmelade?**

January
der Januar

January is the first month
of the year.

**Der Januar ist der
erste Monat im Jahr.**

jar
das Glas

Jam comes in a jar.

**Marmelade gibt es
im Glas.**

job
die Arbeit

It is a big job.

Das ist viel Arbeit.

juice
der Saft (...saft)

She is pouring a glass of
orange juice.

**Sie gießt ein Glas
Orangensaft ein.**

July
der Juli

The month after
June is July.

**Der Monat nach dem
Juni ist der Juli.**

to jump
springen

The animal loves to jump.

**Das Tier springt sehr
gern.**

June
der Juni

The month after May
is June.

**Der Monat nach dem
Mai ist der Juni.**

junk
das Gerümpel

No one can use this junk.

**Niemand kann dieses
Gerümpel brauchen.**

kangaroo *See Animals (page 10).*
das Känguru *Siehe Tiere (Seite 10).*

to keep
behalten

I want to keep him.

Ich möchte ihn behalten.

key
der Schlüssel

Which key opens the lock?

Welcher Schlüssel öffnet das Schloss?

to kick
treten

He wants to kick the ball.

Er will den Ball treten.

kind
freundlich

She is kind to animals.

Sie ist freundlich zu Tieren.

kind
die Art

What kind of animal is that?

Was für eine Art von Tier ist das?

king
der König

The king is having fun.

Der König hat Spaß.

kiss
der Kuss

Would you like to give the monkey a kiss?

Möchtest du dem Affen einen Kuss geben?

kitchen *See Rooms in a House (page 86).*
die Küche *Siehe Räume in einem Haus (Seite 86).*

kite
der Drachen

Kites can fly high.

Drachen können hoch steigen.

kitten
das Kätzchen

A kitten is a baby cat.

Ein Kätzchen ist ein Katzenbaby.

knee *See People (page 76).*
das Knie *Siehe Menschen (Seite 76).*

knife
das Messer

A knife can cut things.

Ein Messer kann Dinge schneiden.

to knock
klopfen

He starts to knock on the door.

Er beginnt, an die Tür zu klopfen.

to know
wissen

He wants to know what it says.

Er möchte wissen, was darauf steht.

ladder
die Leiter

He climbs the ladder.

Er steigt die Leiter hoch.

lake
der See

He is drinking the lake!

Er trinkt ja den See!

lamp
die Lampe

He has a lamp on his head.

Er hat eine Lampe auf dem Kopf.

lap
der Schoß

He sits on his grandma's lap to hear the story.

Er sitzt auf dem Schoß seiner Großmutter, um die Geschichte zu hören.

last
zuletzt

The pink one is last in line.

Die Rosarote ist zuletzt in der Schlange.

late
spät

It is late at night.

Es ist spät in der Nacht.

to laugh
lachen

It is fun to laugh.

Es macht Spaß zu lachen.

laundry room
die Waschküche

See Rooms in a House (page 86).

Siehe Räume in einem Haus (Seite 86).

lazy
faul

He is so lazy.

Er ist so faul.

leaf
das Blatt

The tree has one leaf.

Der Baum hat ein Blatt.

to leave
fortgehen

She does not want
to leave.

**Sie will nicht
fortgehen.**

left
linke

This is your left hand.

**Dies ist deine
linke Hand.**

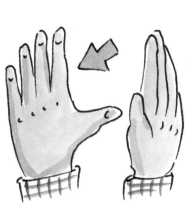

leg
das Bein

See People (page 76).

Siehe Menschen (Seite 76).

lemon
die Zitrone

She likes lemons.

Sie mag Zitronen.

leopard
der Leopard

One leopard is losing
its spots.

**Ein Leopard verliert
seine Flecken.**

to let
lassen

Papa is not going to let
him go.

**Papa will ihn nicht
gehen lassen.**

letter
der Brief

This letter is going
airmail.

**Dieser Brief wird
mit Luftpost verschickt.**

library
die Bücherei

The library is full
of books.

**Die Bücherei ist voll
mit Büchern.**

to lick
lecken

You have to lick it.

**Du musst daran
lecken!**

life
das Leben

Life is wonderful!

**Das Leben ist
wunderschön!**

light
das Licht

The sun gives us light.

Die Sonne schenkt uns Licht.

lightning
der Blitz

Look! There's lightning!

Schau mal! Da ist ein Blitz!

to like
mögen

He is going to like the cake.

Er wird den Kuchen mögen.

like
wie

She looks like a rock.

Sie sieht wie ein Stein aus.

line
der Strich

I can draw a line.

Ich kann einen Strich zeichnen.

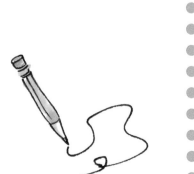

lion *See Animals (page 10).*
der Löwe *Siehe Tiere (Seite 10).*

to listen
hören (...hören)

He does not want to listen to loud music.

Er möchte sich keine laute Musik anhören.

little
klein

The bug is little.

Der Käfer ist klein.

to live
leben

What a nice place to live!

Was für ein schöner Platz zum Leben!

living room *See Rooms in a House (page 86).*
das Wohnzimmer *Siehe Räume in einem Haus (Seite 86).*

llama *See Animals (page 10).*
das Lama *Siehe Tiere (Seite 10).*

to lock
abschließen
(...zu...)

Do not forget to lock the door.

Vergiss nicht, die Tür abzuschließen.

long
lang

That is a long snake.

Das ist eine lange Schlange.

to look
ansehen
(...zu...)

I use this to look at stars.

Ich benutze es, um mir die Sterne anzusehen.

to lose
verlieren

He does not want to lose his hat.

Er möchte seine Mütze nicht verlieren.

lost, to be
sich verlaufen

Oh, no! He is lost.

O je! Er hat sich verlaufen.

lots
viele

There are lots of bubbles.

Es gibt viele Seifenblasen.

loud
laut

The music is loud!

Die Musik ist laut!

to love
lieben

She is going to love the present.

Sie wird das Geschenk lieben.

love
die Liebe

Love is wonderful.

Liebe ist wunderschön.

low
niedrig

The bridge is low.

Die Brücke ist niedrig.

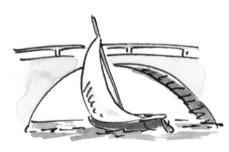

lunch
das Mittagessen

He has nuts for lunch.

Er hat Nüsse zum Mittagessen.

mad
wütend

The frogs are mad.

Die Frösche sind wütend.

mail
die Post

The mail is here.

Die Post ist da.

mailbox
der Briefkasten

What is in that mailbox?

Was ist denn in dem Briefkasten?

mail carrier
der Briefträger

Our mail carrier brings us the mail.

Unser Briefträger bringt uns die Post.

to make
machen

A belt is easy to make.

Einen Gürtel kann man einfach machen.

man
der Mann

The man is waving.

Der Mann winkt.

mango
die Mango

Is he going to eat the whole mango?

Wird er die Mango ganz aufessen?

mantis *See Insects (page 52).*
die Gottesanbeterin *Siehe Insekten (Seite 52).*

many
viele

There are many dots!

Es gibt viele Punkte!

map
die Landkarte

The map shows where to go.

Die Landkarte zeigt, wohin der Weg geht.

maraca
die Maraca

Shake those maracas!

Schüttle die Maracas!

March
der März

The month after
February is March.

**Der Monat nach dem
Februar ist der März.**

math
das Rechnen

He is not very good
at math.

**Er ist nicht sehr
gut im Rechnen.**

May
der Mai

The month after April
is May.

**Der Monat nach dem
April ist der Mai.**

maybe
vielleicht

Maybe it is a ball.

**Vielleicht ist es
ein Ball.**

mayor
der
Bürgermeister

The mayor leads
the town.

**Der Bürgermeister
regiert die Stadt.**

me
mich

Look at me!

Schau mich an!

to mean
bedeuten

That has to mean "hello."

**Das bedeutet
bestimmt:
„Guten Tag!"**

meat
das Fleisch

I am eating meat, salad,
and potatoes for dinner.

**Ich esse Fleisch,
Salat und Kartoffeln
zum Abendessen.**

medicine
die Medizin

Take your medicine!

**Nimm deine
Medizin ein!**

to meet
kennenlernen
(...zu...)

I am happy to meet you.

Es freut mich, Sie kennenzulernen.

meow
miau

Cats say, "MEOW!"

Katzen sagen: „MIAU!"

mess
die Unordnung

What a mess!

Was für eine Unordnung!

messy
unordentlich

The bear is a little messy.

Der Bär ist ein bisschen unordentlich.

milk
die Milch

He likes milk.

Er mag Milch.

minute
die Minute

It is one minute before noon.

Es ist eine Minute vor zwölf Uhr mittags.

mirror
der Spiegel

He loves to look in the mirror.

Er schaut sehr gern in den Spiegel.

to miss
verpassen

He does not want to miss the airplane.

Er will das Flugzeug nicht verpassen.

mittens *See Clothing (page 24).*
die Faüstlinge *Siehe Kleidung (Seite 24).*

to mix
vermischen

Use the spoon to mix it.

Nimm den Löffel, um es zu vermischen.

mom
die Mutti

She is the baby's mom.

Das ist die Mutti des Babys.

Monday
der Montag

On Monday, we take baths.

Am Montag baden wir.

money
das Geld

Look at all the money!

Schau dir all das Geld an!

monkey *See Animals (page 10).*
der Affe *Siehe Tiere (Seite 10).*

month
der Monat

January and February are the first two months of the year.

Der Januar und der Februar sind die beiden ersten Monate im Jahr.

moon
der Mond

The moon is up in the sky.

Der Mond ist oben am Himmel.

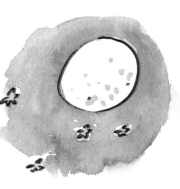

more
mehr

She needs to buy more juice.

Sie muss mehr Saft kaufen.

morning
der Morgen

The sun comes up in the morning.

Die Sonne geht am Morgen auf.

mosquito *See Insects (page 52).*
die Mücke *Siehe Insekten (Seite 52).*

most
meiste

Most of the milk is gone.

Die meiste Milch ist weg.

moth *See Insects (page 52).*
die Motte *Siehe Insekten (Seite 52).*

mother
die Mutter

She is the baby's mother.

**Das ist die Mutter
des Babys.**

motorcycle *See Transportation (page 108).*
das Motorrad *Siehe Transport (Seite 108).*

mountain
der Berg

He is climbing up
the mountain.

**Er steigt den Berg
hinauf.**

mouse
die Maus

The mouse is skating.

**Die Maus läuft
Schlittschuh.**

mouth *See People (page 76).*
der Mund *Siehe Menschen (Seite 76).*

to move
umziehen

They have to move.

Sie müssen umziehen.

movie
der Film

They are watching
a movie.

**Sie sehen sich
einen Film an.**

Mr.
Herr

Say hello to Mr. Green.

**Sagen Sie: „Guten Tag,
Herr Grün!"**

Mrs.
Frau

Mrs. English is getting
on the bus.

**Frau Englisch steigt
in den Bus.**

much
viel

There is not much in
the refrigerator.

**Es ist nicht viel im
Kühlschrank.**

music
die Musik

They can play music.

**Sie können Musik
spielen.**

my
mein

This is my nose.

**Dies ist meine
Nase.**

N

nail
der Nagel

Try to hit the nail!

Versuch mal, den Nagel zu treffen!

name
der Name

His name begins with "R".

Sein Name beginnt mit „R".

neck *See People (page 76).*
der Hals *Siehe Menschen (Seite 76).*

necklace
die Kette

She loves her necklace.

Sie liebt ihre Kette.

to need
brauchen

He is going to need a snack later.

Er wird später einen Snack brauchen.

neighbor
der Nachbar

They are neighbors.

Das sind Nachbarn.

nest
das Nest

The birds are near their nest.

Die Vögel sind nahe bei ihrem Nest.

never
niemals

She is never going to fly.

Sie wird niemals fliegen.

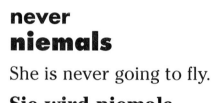

new
neu

He has a new umbrella.

Er hat einen neuen Regenschirm.

newspaper
die Zeitung

Who is cutting my newspaper?

Wer zerschneidet meine Zeitung?

next
neben

She is next to the rock.

Sie ist neben dem Stein.

next
nächste

The horse is next.

Das Pferd ist der Nächste.

nice
nett

What a nice clown!

Was für ein netter Clown!

night
die Nacht

It is dark at night.

In der Nacht ist es dunkel.

nine *See Numbers and Colors (page 68).*
neun *Siehe Zahlen und Farben (Seite 68).*

nineteen *See Numbers and Colors (page 68).*
neunzehn *Siehe Zahlen und Farben (Seite 68).*

ninety *See Numbers and Colors (page 68).*
neunzig *Siehe Zahlen und Farben (Seite 68).*

no
nein

No, you may not go.

Nein, du darfst nicht gehen.

noise
der Lärm

He is making a terrible noise.

Er macht einen schrecklichen Lärm.

noisy
laut

They are very noisy.

Sie sind sehr laut.

noon
der Mittag

It is noon.

Es ist Mittag.

Numbers and Colors
Zahlen und Farben

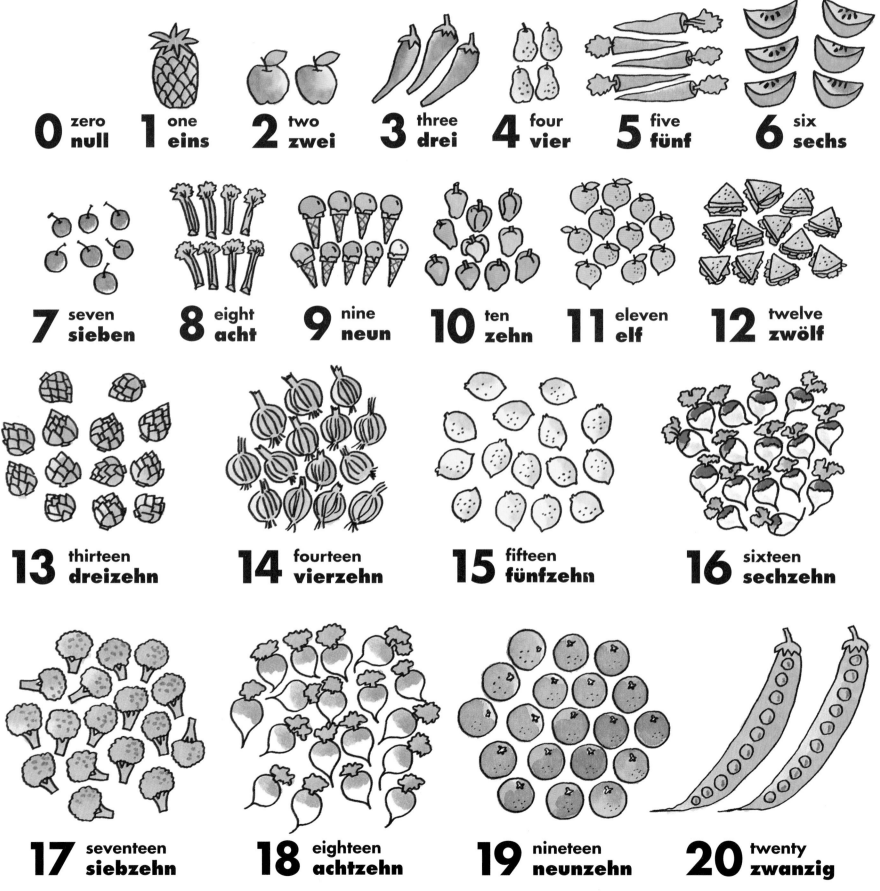

0 zero null

1 one eins

2 two zwei

3 three drei

4 four vier

5 five fünf

6 six sechs

7 seven sieben

8 eight acht

9 nine neun

10 ten zehn

11 eleven elf

12 twelve zwölf

13 thirteen dreizehn

14 fourteen vierzehn

15 fifteen fünfzehn

16 sixteen sechzehn

17 seventeen siebzehn

18 eighteen achtzehn

19 nineteen neunzehn

20 twenty zwanzig

30 thirty
dreißig

40 forty
vierzig

50 fifty
fünfzig

60 sixty
sechzig

70 seventy
siebzig

80 eighty
achtzig

90 ninety
neunzig

100 one hundred
einhundert

1000 one thousand
eintausend

Colors

Farben

black
schwarz

blue
blau

brown
braun

gray
grau

green
grün

orange
orange

pink
rosa

purple
lila

red
rot

tan
beige

white
weiß

yellow
gelb

north
der Norden

It is cold in the north.

Im Norden ist es kalt.

nose *See People (page 76).*
die Nase *Siehe Menschen (Seite 76).*

not
nicht

The bird is not red.

Der Vogel ist nicht rot.

note
die Notiz

He is writing a note.

Er schreibt sich eine Notiz auf.

nothing
nichts

There is nothing in the bottle.

In der Flasche ist nichts.

November
der November

The month after October is November.

Der Monat nach dem Oktober ist der November.

now
jetzt

The mouse needs to run now.

Jetzt muss die Maus schnell laufen.

number
die Zahl

There are five numbers.

Hier sind fünf Zahlen.

nurse
die Krankenschwester

She wants to be a nurse.

Sie möchte Krankenschwester werden.

nut
die Nuss

I think he likes nuts.

Ich glaube, er mag Nüsse.

ocean
der Ozean

This turtle swims in the ocean.

Diese Schildkröte schwimmt im Ozean.

o'clock
Uhr

It is one o'clock.

Es ist ein Uhr.

October
der Oktober

The month after September is October.

Der Monat nach dem September ist der Oktober.

of
von

The color of the airplane is yellow.

Die Farbe von dem Flugzeug ist gelb.

office
See Rooms in a House (page 86).
das Arbeitszimmer
Siehe Räume in einem Haus (Seite 86).

oh
oh

Oh! What a surprise!

Oh! Was für eine Überraschung!

old
alt

The alligator is very old.

Der Alligator ist sehr alt.

on
auf

The coat is on the chair.

Der Mantel ist auf dem Stuhl.

71

once
einmal

Birthdays come once a year.

Geburtstage gibt es einmal im Jahr.

one *See Numbers and Colors (page 68).*
eins *Siehe Zahlen und Farben (Seite 68).*

onion
die Zwiebel

He is chopping an onion.

Er hackt eine Zwiebel.

only
nur

This is the only food left.

Nur das ist noch an Essen übrig.

open
offen

The window is open.

Das Fenster ist offen.

or
oder

Do you want the red one or the blue one?

Nimmst du das rote oder das blaue?

orange *See Numbers and Colors (page 68).*
orange *Siehe Zahlen und Farben (Seite 68).*

orange
die Apfelsine

He is squeezing oranges.

Er presst Apfelsinen aus.

ostrich
der Strauß

An ostrich can run fast.

Ein Strauß kann schnell laufen.

other
andere

What is on the other side?

Was gibt es auf der anderen Seite?

oven
der Backofen

We bake cookies in an oven.

Plätzchen backen wir in einem Backofen.

ouch
autsch

Ouch! That hurts!

Autsch! Das tut weh!

over
über

She is holding the umbrella over her head.

Sie hält den Regenschirm über ihren Kopf.

out
hinaus

He goes out.

Er geht hinaus.

owl
die Eule

The owl does not sleep at night.

Die Eule schläft nicht bei Nacht.

outdoors
draußen

We like to play outdoors.

Wir spielen gern draußen.

to own
besitzen

It is wonderful to own a book.

Es ist wunderbar, ein Buch zu besitzen.

P

page
die Seite

He is turning the page.

Er blättert die Seite um.

paint
die Farbe

The baby is playing with paint.

Das Baby spielt mit Farbe.

painter
der Maler

He is a painter.

Er ist Maler.

pajamas
der Schlafanzug

She is wearing pajamas to sleep.

Sie trägt einen Schlafanzug zum Schlafen.

pan
die Pfanne

We cook in a pan.

Mit einer Pfanne braten wir.

panda
der Panda

This panda is hungry.

Dieser Panda ist hungrig.

pants
die Hosen *See Clothing (page 24).* *Siehe Kleidung (Seite 24).*

paper
das Papier

Write on the paper!

Schreib auf das Papier!

parents
die Eltern

These parents have many babies.

Diese Eltern haben viele Babys.

park
der Park

We like to go to the park.

Wir gehen gern zum Park.

parrot
der Papagei

This parrot can say,
"Cracker!"

**Dieser Papagei kann
„Kräcker!" sagen.**

part
das Teil

A wheel is part of the car.

**Ein Rad ist ein Teil
des Autos.**

party
die Party

The ants are having
a party.

**Die Ameisen
machen eine Party.**

to pat
streicheln

The baby tries to pat
the dog.

**Das Baby versucht,
den Hund zu
streicheln.**

paw
die Pfote

He wants to shake paws.

**Er möchte ihm die
Pfote schütteln.**

pea
die Erbse

He does not like to
eat peas.

**Er isst nicht
gern Erbsen.**

peach
der Pfirsich

Peaches grow on trees.

**Pfirsiche wachsen
an Bäumen.**

pen
der Füller

The pen is leaking.

Der Füller läuft aus.

pencil
der Bleistift

A pencil is for drawing.

**Ein Bleistift ist zum
Zeichnen da.**

Menschen • Dein Körper

head
der Kopf

face
das Gesicht

stomach
der Bauch

knee
das Knie

foot
der Fuß

leg
das Bein

eye
das Auge

thumb
der Daumen

hair
das Haar

arm
der Arm

neck
der Hals

finger
der Finger

hand
die Hand

76

ear
das Ohr

tooth
der Zahn

to see
sehen

nose
die Nase

to touch
berühren

mouth
der Mund

toe
der Zeh

to smell
riechen

to hear
hören

to taste
schmecken

penguin
der Pinguin

There is a penguin in your sink.

In deinem Waschbecken ist ein Pinguin.

people
die Leute

These people are going up.

Diese Leute fahren nach oben.

pepper
der Pfeffer

She is using too much pepper.

Sie nimmt zu viel Pfeffer.

peppers
die Paprikaschoten

Peppers are good to eat.

Paprikaschoten sind gesund.

perfume
das Parfüm

She is wearing perfume.

Sie trägt Parfüm.

pet
das Haustier

The pig is a pet.

Dieses Schwein ist ein Haustier.

photograph
das Foto

Look at the photograph!

Schau dir das Foto an!

piano
das Klavier

He plays the piano very well.

Er spielt sehr gut Klavier.

to pick
pflücken

This dog likes to pick berries.

Dieser Hund pflückt gern Beeren.

picnic
das Picknick

They are having a picnic.

Sie machen ein Picknick.

picture
das Bild

This is a picture of a rabbit.

Dies ist ein Bild von einem Kaninchen.

pie
der Kuchen

Who is eating the pie?

Wer (fr)isst denn den Kuchen?

pig *See Animals (page 10).*
das Schwein *Siehe Tiere (Seite 10).*

pillow
das Kopfkissen

A pillow is for sleeping.

Ein Kopfkissen ist zum Schlafen da.

ping-pong *See Games and Sports (page 44).*
das Tischtennis *Siehe Spiele und Sportarten (Seite 44).*

pink *See Numbers and Colors (page 68).*
rosa *Siehe Zahlen und Farben (Seite 68).*

pizza
die Pizza

We like to eat pizza.

Wir essen gern Pizza.

to place
setzen

It is good to place glasses on the nose.

Es ist gut, die Brille auf die Nase zu setzen.

to plan
planen (...planen)

It helps to plan ahead.

Es hilft vorauszuplanen.

to plant
pflanzen

He likes to plant nuts.

Er pflanzt gern Nüsse.

to play
spielen

Do you want to play with us?

Willst du mit uns spielen?

playground
der Spielplatz

Meet me at the
playground!

**Triff mich auf dem
Spielplatz!**

playroom
das Spielzimmer

See Rooms in a House (page 86).

*Siehe Räume in
einem Haus (Seite 86).*

please
bitte

Please, feed me!

**Bitte, füttere
mich doch!**

pocket
die Tasche

What is in his pocket?

**Was ist denn in
seiner Tasche?**

point
die Spitze

It has a sharp point.
Ouch!

**Sie hat eine scharfe
Spitze. Autsch!**

to point
mit dem Finger zeigen

It is not polite to point.

**Es ist nicht höflich,
mit dem Finger zu
zeigen.**

police officer
die Polizistin

The police officer helps
us cross the street.

**Die Polizistin hilft
uns, die Straße zu
überqueren.**

police station
das Polizeirevier

You can get help at
the police station.

**Man kann auf
dem Polizeirevier
Hilfe holen.**

polite
höflich

He is so polite!

Er ist so höflich!

pond
der Teich

She falls into the pond.

Sie fällt in den Teich.

poor
arm

This poor monkey does not have much money.

Dieser arme Affe hat nicht viel Geld.

porch   *See Rooms in a House (page 86).*
die Veranda   *Siehe Räume in einem Haus (Seite 86).*

post office
die Post

Letters go to the post office.

Briefe müssen zur Post.

pot
der Topf

It is time to stir the pot.

Es ist Zeit, im Topf zu rühren.

potato
die Kartoffel

These potatoes have eyes.

Diese Kartoffeln haben Augen.

to pound
einhämmern (...zu...)

Use a hammer to pound a nail.

Nimm einen Hammer, um einen Nagel einzuhämmern.

present
das Geschenk

Is the present for me?

Ist das Geschenk für mich?

pretty
hübsch

It is not a pretty face.

Das ist kein hübsches Gesicht.

prince
der Prinz

The prince is with his father.

Der Prinz ist mit seinem Vater zusammen.

princess
die Prinzessin

This princess has big feet.

Diese Prinzessin hat große Füße.

81

prize
der Preis

Look who wins the prize.

Schau mal, wer den Preis gewinnt.

purse
die Handtasche

The purse is full.

Die Handtasche ist voll.

proud
stolz

She is proud of her new hat.

Sie ist auf ihren neuen Hut stolz.

to push
drücken

He needs to push hard.

Er muss kräftig drücken.

to pull
ziehen

We're trying to pull him up.

Wir versuchen, ihn nach oben zu ziehen.

to put
stecken

We tell her it is better not to put her foot in her mouth.

Wir sagen ihr, es ist besser, den Fuß nicht in den Mund zu stecken.

puppy
das Hündchen

The puppy is wet.

Das Hündchen ist nass.

puzzle
das Puzzle

Can you put the puzzle together?

Kannst du das Puzzle zusammensetzen?

purple *See Numbers and Colors (page 68).*
lila *Siehe Zahlen und Farben (Seite 68).*

quack
quak

"Quack, quack, quack!"
sing the ducks.

„Quak, quak, quak!"
singen die Enten.

to quarrel
streiten

We do not like to quarrel.

Wir streiten uns
nicht gern.

quarter
das Viertel

A quarter of the pie
is gone.

Ein Viertel vom
Kuchen ist
verschwunden.

queen
die Königin

She is queen of the
zebras.

Sie ist die Königin
der Zebras.

question
die Frage

She has a question.

Sie hat eine Frage.

quick
schnell

A rabbit is quick; a
tortoise is slow.

Ein Kaninchen ist
schnell. Eine
Schildkröte ist
langsam.

quiet
still

Shh! Be quiet!

Psst! Seid still!

quilt
die Bettdecke

Who is under the quilt?

Wer ist denn unter
der Bettdecke?

to quit
aufhören

The raccoon wants to
quit practicing.

Der Waschbär
möchte mit dem
Üben aufhören.

quite
ziemlich

It is quite cold today.

Es ist heute
ziemlich kalt.

R

rabbit *See Animals (page 10).*
das Kaninchen *Siehe Tiere (Seite 10).*

race
das Rennen

Who is going to win
the race?

**Wer wird wohl das
Rennen gewinnen?**

radio
das Radio

They listen to the radio.

Sie hören Radio.

rain
der Regen

She likes the rain.

Sie mag den Regen.

rainbow
der Regenbogen

She is standing in a
rainbow.

**Sie steht in einem
Regenbogen.**

raincoat *See Clothing (page 24).*
der Regenmantel *Siehe Kleidung
(Seite 24).*

raindrop
der Regentropfen

Look at the raindrops.

**Schau dir die
Regentropfen an.**

raining
regnen

He is wet because
it is raining.

**Er ist nass, weil
es regnet.**

to read
lesen

Does he know how
to read?

**Weiß er, wie
man liest?**

ready
fertig

The baby is not ready
to go.

**Das Baby ist noch
nicht zum
Ausgehen fertig.**

real
echt

It is not a real dog.

Das ist kein echter Hund.

really
wirklich

She is really tall!

Sie ist wirklich groß!

red
rot

See Numbers and Colors (page 68).

Siehe Zahlen und Farben (Seite 68).

refrigerator
der Kühlschrank

We keep our snowballs in the refrigerator.

Wir heben unsere Schneebälle im Kühlschrank auf.

to remember
sich erinnern

It is hard to remember his phone number.

Es ist schwer, sich an seine Telefonnummer zu erinnern.

restaurant
das Restaurant

She is eating at a restaurant.

Sie isst im Restaurant.

rice
der Reis

Where is all the rice?

Wo ist denn der ganze Reis?

rich
reich

He is very rich.

Er ist sehr reich.

to ride
reiten

It is fun to ride on a horse.

Es macht Spaß, auf einem Pferd zu reiten.

right
rechte

This is your right hand.

Dies ist deine rechte Hand.

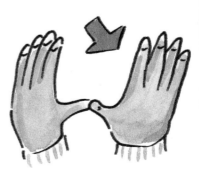

closet
der Schrank

office
das Arbeitszimmer

bedroom
das Schlafzimmer

living room
das Wohnzimmer

hall
der Flur

porch
die Veranda

basement
der Keller

laundry room
die Waschküche

ring
der Ring

She has a new ring.

Sie hat einen neuen Ring.

to ring
läuten

The telephone is going to ring soon.

Das Telefon wird bald läuten.

river
der Fluss

I am floating down the river.

Ich treibe den Fluss hinunter.

road
die Straße

The road goes over the hill.

Die Straße geht über den Hügel.

robot
der Roboter

A robot is looking in my window!

Ein Roboter schaut in mein Fenster!

rock
der Felsen

What went around the rock?

Was ist denn um den Felsen gelaufen?

roof
das Dach

There is a cow on the roof.

Auf dem Dach ist eine Kuh.

room
das Zimmer

The little house has little rooms.

Das kleine Haus hat kleine Zimmer.

rooster *See Animals (page 10).*
der Hahn *Siehe Tiere (Seite 10).*

root
die Wurzel

The plant has
deep roots.

**Die Pflanze hat
tiefe Wurzeln.**

rose
die Rose

She likes roses.

Sie mag Rosen.

round
rund

These things
are round.

**Diese Dinge sind
rund.**

to rub
reiben

It is fun to rub
his tummy.

**Es macht Spaß,
seinen Bauch
zu reiben.**

rug
der Teppich

A bug is on the rug.

**Ein Käfer ist auf
dem Teppich.**

to run
laufen

You need feet to run!

**Man braucht Füße,
um zu laufen!**

running *See Sports and Games (page 44).*
das Laufen *Siehe Spiele und Sportarten
(Seite 44).*

S

sad
traurig

This is a sad face.

Das ist ein trauriges Gesicht.

sailboat   *See Transportation (page 108).*
das Segelboot   *Siehe Transport (Seite 108).*

salad
der Salat

He is making a salad.

Er macht einen Salat.

salt
das Salz

She is using too much salt.

Sie nimmt zu viel Salz.

same
gleich

They look the same.

Sie sehen gleich aus.

sand
der Sand

There is so much sand at the beach.

Es gibt so viel Sand am Strand.

sandwich
das Butterbrot

It's a pickle sandwich! Yum!

Ein Butterbrot mit sauren Gurken! Lecker!

sandy
sandig

The beach is sandy.

Der Strand ist sandig.

Saturday
der Samstag

On Saturday, we work together.

Am Samstag arbeiten wir zusammen.

sausage
die Wurst

This dog likes sausages.

Dieser Hund mag Würste.

saw
die Säge

A saw is for cutting.

Eine Säge ist zum Schneiden da.

to say
sagen

She wants to say hello.

Sie möchte dir Guten Tag sagen.

scarf *See Clothing (page 24).*
der Schal *Siehe Kleidung (Seite 24).*

school
die Schule

He can learn in school.

Er kann in der Schule lernen.

scissors
die Schere

Look what he is cutting with the scissors.

Schau mal, was er mit der Schere ausschneidet!

to scrub
schrubben

He wants to scrub the tub.

Er will die Wanne schrubben.

sea
das Meer

Whales live in the sea.

Wale leben im Meer.

seat
der Sitz

The seat is too high.

Der Sitz ist zu hoch.

secret
das Geheimnis

She is telling a secret.

Sie verrät ein Geheimnis.

to see *See People (page 76).*
sehen *Siehe Menschen (Seite 76).*

seed
der Samen

When you plant a seed,
it grows.

**Wenn du einen
Samen pflanzt, wächst er.**

to sell
verkaufen

He has many balloons
to sell.

**Er hat viele Ballons
zu verkaufen.**

to send
schicken

Mom has to send a
letter in the mail.

**Mutti muss einen
Brief mit der
Post schicken.**

September
der September

The month after August
is September.

**Der Monat nach
dem August ist
der September.**

seven *See Numbers and Colors (page 68).*
sieben *Siehe Zahlen und Farben (Seite 68).*

seventeen *See Numbers and Colors (page 68).*
siebzehn *Siehe Zahlen und Farben (Seite 68).*

seventy *See Numbers and Colors (page 68).*
siebzig *Siehe Zahlen und Farben (Seite 68).*

shark
der Hai

A shark has many teeth.

**Ein Hai hat viele
Zähne.**

shawl *See Clothing (page 24).*
das Umhängetuch *Siehe Kleidung (Seite 24).*

she
sie

She is hiding.

Sie versteckt sich.

sheep *See Animals (page 10).*
das Schaf *Siehe Tiere (Seite 10).*

shirt *See Clothing (page 24).*
das Hemd *Siehe Kleidung (Seite 24).*

shoes *See Clothing (page 24).*
die Schuhe *Siehe Kleidung (Seite 24).*

to shop
einkaufen

He likes to shop.

Er kauft gern ein.

short
klein

He is too short.

Er ist zu klein.

to shout
schreien

They have to shout.

Sie müssen schreien.

shovel
die Schaufel

She needs a bigger shovel.

Sie braucht eine größere Schaufel.

show
die Aufführung

They are in a show.

Sie sind in einer Aufführung.

to show
zeigen

Open wide to show your new tooth!

Mach weit auf, um deinen neuen Zahn zu zeigen!

shy
schüchtern

He is very shy.

Er ist sehr schüchtern.

sick
krank

The poor rhinoceros is sick!

Das arme Nashorn ist krank!

side
die Seite

The tree is on the side of the house.

Der Baum steht an der Seite vom Haus.

sidewalk
der Bürgersteig

They are playing on the sidewalk.

Sie spielen auf dem Bürgersteig.

sign
das Schild

This is the bakery's sign.

Dies ist das Schild der Bäckerei.

silly
verrückt

He has a silly smile.

**Er hat ein
verrücktes Grinsen.**

to sing
singen

She loves to sing.

Sie singt sehr gern.

sister
die Schwester

They are sisters.

Das sind Schwestern.

to sit
sitzen

They want to sit.

Sie möchten sitzen.

six   *See Numbers and Colors (page 68).*
sechs   *Siehe Zahlen und Farben (Seite 68).*

sixteen   *See Numbers and Colors (page 68).*
sechzehn   *Siehe Zahlen und Farben (Seite 68).*

sixty   *See Numbers and Colors (page 68).*
sechzig   *Siehe Zahlen und Farben (Seite 68).*

skateboard   *See Transportation (page 108).*
das Skateboard   *Siehe Transport (Seite 108).*

skates   *See Transportation (page 108).*
die Rollschuhe   *Siehe Transport (Seite 108).*

skating (ice)   *See Games and Sports (page 44).*
das Schlittschuhlaufen
   Siehe Spiele und Sportarten (Seite 44).

skiing   *See Games and Sports (page 44).*
das Skilaufen   *Siehe Spiele und Sportarten (Seite 44).*

skirt   *See Clothing (page 24).*
der Rock   *Siehe Kleidung (Seite 24).*

sky
der Himmel

The sky is full of stars.

**Der Himmel ist voll
von Sternen.**

to sleep
schlafen gehen

He is ready to sleep.

**Er ist fertig, schlafen
zu gehen.**

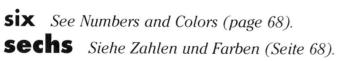

slow
langsam

A rabbit is quick;
a tortoise is slow.

**Ein Kaninchen ist
schnell. Eine
Schildkröte ist
langsam.**

small
klein

An ant is small.

**Eine Ameise
ist klein.**

to smell *See People (page 76).*
riechen *Siehe Menschen (Seite 76).*

smile
das Lächeln

What a big smile!

**Was für ein großes
Lächeln!**

smoke
der Rauch

Watch out for
the smoke!

**Nimm dich vor
dem Rauch in Acht!**

snail
die Schnecke

He has a snail on
his nose.

**Er hat eine
Schnecke auf
der Nase.**

snake *See Animals (page 10).*
die Schlange *Siehe Tiere (Seite 10).*

sneakers *See Clothing (page 24).*
die Turnschuhe *Siehe Kleidung (Seite 24).*

to snore
schnarchen

Try not to snore.

**Versuch, nicht zu
schnarchen!**

snow
der Schnee

Snow is white and cold.

**Schnee ist weiß
und kalt.**

snowball
der Schneeball

He is throwing
snowballs.

**Er wirft
Schneebälle.**

so
so

She is so tall!

Sie ist so groß!

soap
die Seife

He is using soap
to wash.

**Er benutzt Seife
zum Waschen.**

soccer *See Games and Sports (page 44).*
der Fußball *Siehe Spiele und Sportarten (Seite 44).*

socks *See Clothing (page 24).*
die Socken *Siehe Kleidung (Seite 24).*

sofa
das Sofa

The zebras are sitting
on the sofa.

**Die Zebras sitzen
auf dem Sofa.**

some
einige

Some of them are pink.

**Einige von ihnen
sind rosa.**

someday
eines Tages

Dad says I can
drive . . . someday.

**Vati sagt, ich darf
fahren . . . eines
Tages.**

someone
jemand

Someone is behind
the fence.

**Jemand ist hinter
dem Zaun.**

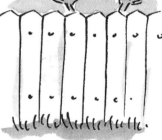

something
etwas

Something is under
the rug.

**Etwas ist unter
dem Teppich.**

song
das Lied

A song is for singing.

**Ein Lied ist zum
Singen da.**

soon
bald

Soon it is going to
be noon.

Bald ist es Mittag.

sorry, to be
Leid tun

She is sorry she dropped it.

Es tut ihr Leid, dass sie es fallen lassen hat.

soup
die Suppe

The soup is hot!

Die Suppe ist heiß!

south
der Süden

It is warm in the south.

Im Süden ist es warm.

special
besonderes

This is a special car.

Dies ist ein besonderes Auto.

spider
die Spinne

This spider is friendly.

Diese Spinne ist freundlich.

spoon
der Löffel

A spoon can't run; can it?

Ein Löffel kann doch nicht laufen, oder?

spring
der Frühling

Flowers grow in spring.

Im Frühling wachsen die Blumen.

square
das Quadrat

A square has four sides.

Ein Quadrat hat vier Seiten.

squirrel
das Eichhörnchen

There is a squirrel on that hat!

Auf dem Hut ist ein Eichhörnchen!

stamp
die Briefmarke

A stamp goes on a letter.

Eine Briefmarke gehört auf einen Brief.

to stand
stehen

She does not like
to stand.

Sie steht nicht gern.

star
der Stern

That star is winking.

Dieser Stern funkelt.

to start
anfangen

They want to start
with *A*.

**Sie wollen mit *A*
anfangen.**

to stay
bleiben

He has to stay inside.

**Er muss drinnen
bleiben.**

to step
treten

Try not to step in
the puddle.

**Versuch, nicht in die
Pfütze zu treten!**

stick
der Stock

The dog wants the stick.

**Der Hund will
den Stock.**

sticky
klebrig

That candy is sticky.

**Dieser Bonbon
ist klebrig.**

still
noch

The phone still is
not ringing.

**Das Telefon klingelt
immer noch nicht.**

stomach   *See People (page 76).*
der Bauch   *Siehe Menschen (Seite 76).*

to stop
anhalten

You have to stop
for a red light.

**Bei einer roten
Ampel muss man
anhalten.**

store
das Geschäft

She buys books at
the store.

**Sie kauft Bücher
im Geschäft.**

storm
der Sturm

She does not like
the storm.

**Sie mag den
Sturm nicht.**

student
der Schüler

The students are
all fish.

**Die Schüler sind
alle Fische.**

story
die Geschichte

We all know this story.

**Diese Geschichte
kennen wir alle.**

subway *See Transportation (page 108).*
die Untergrundbahn *Siehe Transport (Seite 108).*

strange
seltsam

This is a strange animal.

**Dies ist ein
seltsames Tier.**

suddenly
plötzlich

Suddenly, it is raining.

Plötzlich regnet es.

strawberry
die Erdbeere

This strawberry is big!

**Diese Erdbeere
ist groß!**

suit
der Anzug

Something is spilling
on his suit.

**Etwas läuft ihm auf
den Anzug.**

street
die Straße

There is an elephant
in the street!

**Auf der Straße ist
ein Elefant!**

suitcase
der Koffer

What is in that suitcase?

**Was ist denn in
dem Koffer da?**

summer
der Sommer

It is warm in summer.

Im Sommer ist es warm.

sun
die Sonne

The sun is hot.

Die Sonne ist heiß.

Sunday
der Sonntag

On Sunday, we eat dinner with Grandma.

Am Sonntag essen wir mit Großmutter zu Abend.

sunflower
die Sonnenblume

The sunflower is big and yellow.

Die Sonnenblume ist groß und gelb.

sunny
sonnig

She loves sunny days.

Sie hat sonnige Tage sehr gern.

sure
sicher

I am sure the door is not going to open.

Ich bin sicher, dass die Tür nicht aufgeht.

surprised
überrascht

She is surprised.

Sie ist überrascht.

sweater *See Clothing (page 24).*
die Strickjacke *Siehe Kleidung (Seite 24).*

to swim
schwimmen

The fish likes to swim.

Der Fisch schwimmt gern.

swimming *See Games and Sports (page 44).*
das Schwimmen *Siehe Spiele und Sportarten (Seite 44).*

table
der Tisch

There is a chicken on the table.

Auf dem Tisch ist ein Huhn.

tail
der Schwanz

He has a long tail.

Er hat einen langen Schwanz.

to take
nehmen (...nehmen)

He is going to take the suitcase with him.

Er wird den Koffer mitnehmen.

to talk
sprechen

They like to talk on the phone.

Sie sprechen gern am Telefon.

tall
groß

The red one is very tall.

Der Rote ist sehr groß.

tambourine
das Tamburin

Shake that tambourine!

Schüttle das Tamburin!

tan *See Numbers and Colors (page 68).*
beige *Siehe Zahlen und Farben (Seite 68).*

to taste *See People (page 76).*
schmecken *Siehe Menschen (Seite 76).*

taxi *See Transportation (page 108).*
das Taxi *Siehe Transport (Seite 108).*

teacher
die Lehrerin

Our teacher helps us to learn.

Unsere Lehrerin hilft uns beim Lernen.

tear
die Träne

There is a tear on her cheek.

Auf ihrer Backe ist eine Träne.

telephone
das Telefon

People can call you on the telephone.

Man kann dich mit dem Telefon anrufen.

television
das Fernsehen

My goldfish likes to watch television.

Mein Goldfisch schaut gern Fernsehen.

tell
sagen

Mom has to tell her the word.

Die Mutti muss ihr das Wort sagen.

ten *See Numbers and Colors (page 68).*
zehn *Siehe Zahlen und Farben (Seite 68).*

tennis *See Games and Sports (page 44).*
das Tennis *Siehe Spiele und Sportarten (Seite 44).*

tent
das Zelt

What is inside the tent?

Was ist im Zelt drinnen?

termite *See Insects (page 52).*
die Termite *Siehe Insekten (Seite 52).*

terrible
schrecklich

What a terrible mess!

Was für eine schreckliche Unordnung!

to thank
danken

He wants to thank the firefighter.

Er möchte dem Feuerwehrmann danken.

that
das

What is that?

Was ist das?

the
der, die, das, des, dem, den

The apple, the banana, and the pears are running away.

Der Apfel, die Banane und die Birnen laufen weg.

their
ihr

They are pointing to their suitcases.

Sie zeigen auf ihre Koffer.

them
ihnen

The shoes belong to them.

Die Schuhe gehören ihnen.

then
dann

Get into bed. Then sleep.

Geh ins Bett! Schlaf dann!

there
dort

There she is!

Dort ist sie!

these
diese

No one wants these eggs.

Diese Eier will niemand.

they
sie

See the mice? They are dancing.

Siehst du die Mäuse? Sie tanzen.

thin
dünn

One clown is thin.

Der eine Clown ist dünn.

thing
das Ding

What is this thing?

Was ist denn dieses Ding?

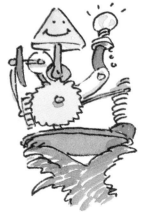

to think
denken

We use our brain to think.

Wir denken mit dem Kopf.

thirsty
durstig

He is thirsty.

Er ist durstig.

thirteen *See Numbers and Colors (page 68).*
dreizehn
Siehe Zahlen und Farben (Seite 68).

thirty *See Numbers and Colors (page 68).*
dreißig
Siehe Zahlen und Farben (Seite 68).

this
dieses

This baby is sad.

Dieses Baby ist traurig.

those
die

Those babies are happy.

Die Babys sind fröhlich.

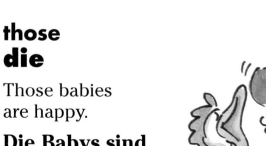

thousand *See Numbers and Colors (page 68).*
tausend
Siehe Zahlen und Farben (Seite 68).

three *See Numbers and Colors (page 68).*
drei
Siehe Zahlen und Farben (Seite 68).

through
durch

The ball is coming through the window.

Der Ball kommt durch das Fenster.

to throw
werfen

We like to throw the ball.

Wir werfen gern den Ball.

thumb *See People (page 76).*
der Daumen
Siehe Menschen (Seite 76).

thunder
der Donner

Thunder is loud.

Donner ist laut.

Thursday
der Donnerstag

On Thursday, we wash clothes.

Am Donnerstag waschen wir Wäsche.

tie *See Clothing (page 24).*
die Krawatte *Siehe Kleidung (Seite 24).*

to tie
binden

Is he going to tie his shoelaces?

Wird er sich die Schnürsenkel binden?

tiger
der Tiger

This is a tiger.

Dies ist ein Tiger.

time
die Zeit

It is time to wash the dishes.

Es wird Zeit zum Geschirrspülen.

tire
der Reifen

One tire is flat.

Ein Reifen ist platt.

tired
müde

She is tired.

Sie ist müde.

to
zur

He is going to school.

Er geht zur Schule.

today
heute

Today is her birthday.

Sie hat heute Geburtstag.

toe *See People (page 76).*
der Zeh *Siehe Menschen (Seite 76).*

together
zusammen

They are sitting together.

Sie sitzen zusammen.

tomato
die Tomate

Mmm! It is a big, juicy tomato.

Mmm! Das ist eine große, saftige Tomate.

tomorrow
morgen

Tomorrow is another day.

Morgen ist auch ein Tag.

tonight
heute Abend

He is sleepy tonight.

Er ist heute Abend schläfrig.

too
auch

The baby is singing, too.

Auch das Baby singt.

tooth *See People (page 76).*
der Zahn *Siehe Menschen (Seite 76).*

toothbrush
die Zahnbürste

My toothbrush is red.

Meine Zahnbürste ist rot.

top
oben

The bird is on top.

Der Vogel ist oben.

to touch *See People (page 76).*
berühren *Siehe Menschen (Seite 76).*

towel
das Handtuch

He needs a towel.

Er braucht ein Handtuch.

town
die Stadt

The ant lives in a town.

Die Ameise lebt in einer Stadt.

tree
der Baum

There is a cow sitting in that tree.

In dem Baum sitzt eine Kuh.

toy
das Spielzeug

He has all kinds of toys.

Er hat alles mögliche Spielzeug.

triangle
das Dreieck

A triangle has three sides.

Ein Dreieck hat drei Seiten.

track
die Spur
(...spur)

That is a rabbit track.

Das ist eine Hasenspur.

to trick
hereinlegen
(...zu...)

Her job is to trick us.

Ihre Aufgabe ist es, uns hereinzulegen.

train *See Transportation (page 108).*
der Zug *Siehe Transport (Seite 108).*

trip
die Reise

She is going on a trip.

Sie macht eine Reise.

treat
der Leckerbissen

A bone is a treat.

Ein Knochen ist ein Leckerbissen.

to trip
hinfallen
(...zu...)

It is no fun to trip.

Es macht keinen Spaß, hinzufallen.

Transportation
Transport

airplane
das Flugzeug

train
der Zug

van
der Lieferwagen

skateboard
das Skateboard

bicycle
das Fahrrad

skates
die Rollschuhe

helicopter
der Hubschrauber

sailboat
das Segelboot

car
das Auto

truck
der Lastwagen

boat
das Boot

subway
die Untergrundbahn

horse
das Pferd

taxi
das Taxi

bus
der Bus

109

truck *See Transportation (page 108).*
der Lastwagen
       Siehe Transport (Seite 108).

trumpet
die Trompete

This is a trumpet.

Dies ist eine Trompete.

to try
versuchen

He wants to try to climb it.

Er will versuchen, hier hoch zu klettern.

Tuesday
der Dienstag

On Tuesday we wash the floors.

Am Dienstag putzen wir die Fußböden.

tulip
die Tulpe

There is a tulip on his head.

Auf seinem Kopf ist eine Tulpe.

to turn
drehen

You have to turn it.

Du musst daran drehen.

turtle
die Schildkröte

That is a fast turtle!

Das ist aber eine schnelle Schildkröte!

twelve *See Numbers and Colors (page 68).*
zwölf *Siehe Zahlen und Farben (Seite 68).*

twenty *See Numbers and Colors (page 68).*
zwanzig *Siehe Zahlen und Farben (Seite 68).*

twins
die Zwillinge

They are twins.

Das sind Zwillinge.

two *See Numbers and Colors (page 68).*
zwei *Siehe Zahlen und Farben (Seite 68).*

ugly
hässlich

Do you think the toad is ugly?

Findest du die Kröte hässlich?

umbrella
der Regenschirm

She has a yellow umbrella.

Sie hat einen gelben Regenschirm.

uncle
der Onkel

My uncle is my dad's brother.

Mein Onkel ist der Bruder meines Vaters.

under
unter

There is something under the bed.

Es ist etwas unter dem Bett.

until
bis

He eats until he is full.

Er isst, bis er satt ist.

up
oben

It is scary up here!

Hier oben ist es aber unheimlich!

upon
auf

The box is upon the box, upon the box.

Die Schachtel ist auf der Schachtel auf der Schachtel.

upside-down
verkehrt herum

He is upside-down.

Er steht verkehrt herum.

us
uns

Come with us!

Kommt doch mit uns!

to use
benutzen

He needs to use a comb.

Er muss einen Kamm benutzen.

V

vacation
der Urlaub

They are on vacation.

Sie machen Urlaub.

vacuum cleaner
der Staubsauger

Here comes the vacuum cleaner!

Hier kommt der Staubsauger!

van *See Transportation (page 108).*
der Lieferwagen *Siehe Transport (Seite 108).*

vegetable
das Gemüse

He likes vegetables.

Er mag Gemüse.

very
sehr

It is very cold in there.

Es ist sehr kalt dort drinnen.

vest *See Clothing (page 24).*
die Weste *Siehe Kleidung (Seite 24).*

veterinarian
die Tierärztin

A veterinarian helps animals.

Eine Tierärztin hilft Tieren.

village
das Dorf

What a pretty village!

Was für ein hübsches Dorf!

violin
die Geige

He is playing the violin.

Er spielt Geige.

to visit
besuchen

He is going to visit Grandma.

Er wird Großmutter besuchen.

volcano
der Vulkan

Don't go near the volcano!

Geh nicht nahe an den Vulkan heran!

to wait
warten

He has to wait
for a bus.

**Er muss auf den
Bus warten.**

to wake up
aufwachen

He is about to
wake up.

**Er wird gleich
aufwachen.**

to walk
laufen

It is good to walk.

Es tut gut zu laufen.

wall
die Mauer

John is building a wall.

**Hans baut eine
Mauer.**

to want
wollen

She is going to
want help.

**Sie wird Hilfe
wollen.**

warm
warm

It is warm by the fire.

**Am Feuer ist
es warm.**

to wash
waschen

It takes a long time to
wash some things.

**Es dauert lange,
manche Sachen
zu waschen.**

wasp   *See Insects (page 52).*
die Wespe   *Siehe Insekten (Seite 52).*

watch
die Uhr

Robert is wearing his
new watch.

**Robert trägt seine
neue Uhr.**

to watch
zuschauen

Peter likes to
watch ants.

**Peter schaut
Ameisen gern zu.**

water
das Wasser

The pool is full of water.

Das Schwimmbad ist voller Wasser.

we
wir

See us? We are all purple.

Siehst du uns? Wir sind alle lila.

weather
das Wetter

What is the weather like today?

Wie ist das Wetter heute?

Wednesday
der Mittwoch

On Wednesday, we go to work.

Am Mittwoch gehen wir zur Arbeit.

week
die Woche

Seven days make a week.

Sieben Tage sind eine Woche.

welcome
willkommen

We are always welcome at Grandma's house.

Bei Großmutter zu Hause sind wir immer willkommen.

well
gut

Thomas builds very well.

Thomas baut sehr gut.

well
gesund

She is not well.

Sie ist nicht gesund.

west
der Westen

The sun goes down in the west.

Die Sonne geht im Westen unter.

wet
nass

William is wet.

Wilhelm ist nass.

what
was

What is outside the window?

Was ist draußen am Fenster?

wheel
das Rad

The bicycle needs a new wheel.

Das Fahrrad braucht ein neues Rad.

when
wenn

When you sleep, you close your eyes.

Wenn du schläfst, machst du die Augen zu.

where
wo

This is where he keeps his dinner.

Hier ist es, wo er sein Abendessen aufbewahrt.

which
welches

Which one do you want?

Welches möchtest du?

while
während

I run while he sleeps.

Ich laufe, während er schläft.

whiskers
die Schnurrhaare

This animal has long whiskers.

Dieses Tier hat lange Schnurrhaare.

to whisper
flüstern

This animal needs to whisper.

Dieses Tier muss flüstern.

whistle
die Pfeife

They can hear the whistle.

Sie können die Pfeife hören.

white   *See Numbers and Colors (page 68).*
weiß   *Siehe Zahlen und Farben (Seite 68).*

who
wer

Who are you?

Wer bist du?

whole
ganz

Can she eat the
whole thing?

**Kann sie das ganze
Ding essen?**

why
warum

Why is the
baby crying?

**Warum weint das
Baby denn?**

wife
die Ehefrau

She is his wife.

**Sie ist seine
Ehefrau.**

wind
der Wind

The wind is blowing.

Der Wind bläst.

window
das Fenster

I can see through
the window.

**Ich kann durchs
Fenster sehen.**

to wink
zwinkern

It is fun to wink.

**Zwinkern macht
Spaß.**

winter
der Winter

He skies in the winter.

**Im Winter läuft
er Ski.**

wish
der Wunsch

The girl has a wish.

**Das Mädchen hat
einen Wunsch.**

with
mit

The cat is dancing
with the dog.

**Die Katze tanzt
mit dem Hund.**

without
ohne

He is going without
his sister.

**Er geht ohne seine
Schwester.**

woman
die Frau

My grandma is a
nice woman.

**Meine Großmutter
ist eine nette Frau.**

wonderful
wunderbar

They are wonderful
dancers.

**Das sind wunderbare
Tänzer.**

woods
der Wald

Someone is walking
in the woods.

**Im Wald geht
jemand spazieren.**

word
das Wort

Do not say a word.

Sag kein Wort!

work
die Arbeit

That is hard work.

**Das ist schwere
Arbeit.**

to work
arbeiten

She has to work
hard today.

**Sie muss heute
schwer arbeiten.**

world
die Welt

The world is beautiful.

Die Welt ist schön.

worried
besorgt

He looks worried.

**Er sieht besorgt
aus.**

to write
schreiben

Katherine is trying to
write with the pencil.

**Katharina versucht,
mit dem Bleistift
zu schreiben.**

wrong
falsch

They are putting on
the wrong hats.

**Sie setzen die
falschen Mützen
auf.**

X-ray
das Röntgenbild

The X-ray shows
his bones.

**Das Röntgenbild
zeigt seine Knochen.**

xylophone
das Xylophon

He's a great xylophone
player.

**Er ist toll am
Xylophon.**

yard
der Garten

There is a dinosaur
in our yard!

**Bei uns im Garten
ist ein Dinosaurier!**

yawn
das Gähnen

What a big yawn!

**Was für ein riesiges
Gähnen!**

year
das Jahr

He runs all year.

**Er läuft das ganze
Jahr hindurch.**

yellow   *See Numbers and Colors (page 68).*
gelb   *Siehe Zahlen und Farben (Seite 68).*

yes
ja

Is he yellow? Yes! He is.

**Ist er gelb? Ja, er
ist gelb.**

yesterday
gestern

Yesterday is the day
before today.

**Gestern ist der Tag
vor heute.**

you
du

You are reading
this book.

**Du liest dieses
Buch.**

your
dein

What color are
your eyes?

**Welche Farbe haben
deine Augen?**

zebra
das Zebra

You cannot have
a pet zebra!

**Du kannst kein
Zebra als Haustier
haben!**

zero
null

See Numbers and Colors (page 68).

Siehe Zahlen und Farben (Seite 68).

zigzag
das Zickzack
(Zickzack...)

The house has zigzags
on it.

**Das Haus hat ein
Zickzackmuster.**

to zip
den Reißverschluss
zumachen

The bee wants to zip
her jacket.

**Die Biene will den
Reißverschluss von
ihrer Jacke zumachen.**

zipper
der
Reißverschluss

The zipper is stuck.

**Der Reißverschluss
klemmt.**

zoo
der Zoo

I can see many animals
at the zoo.

**Im Zoo kann ich
viele Tiere sehen.**

to zoom
schießen

A rocket seems to
zoom into space.

**Eine Rakete scheint
ins Weltall zu
schießen.**

A Family Dinner
Ein Familienessen

**Dinner is ready!
It's time to eat.**
**Das Essen ist fertig!
Es ist Zeit zum Essen.**

**The chicken and vegetables
look delicious.**
**Das Hühnchen und
das Gemüse sehen
lecker aus!**

Here is your napkin.
Hier ist deine Serviette!

Mmmm! They *are* delicious!
**Mmm! Sie *schmecken*
auch lecker!**

**Please pass the salt
and pepper.**
**Kannst du mir bitte
das Salz und den
Pfeffer reichen?**

Dinner is great.
Thanks, Mom.
Das Essen schmeckt toll!
Danke schön, Mutti!

You're welcome, Dear.
Bitte schön, Schatz!

Do you want
more milk?
**Möchtest du noch
etwas Milch?**

No, thank you.
Nein danke!

May I please be excused?
Darf ich bitte aufstehen?

In a few minutes!
But please help us clear
the table first.
**In ein paar Minuten!
Hilf uns aber bitte erst,
den Tisch abzuräumen.**

Of course.
Natürlich!

Meeting and Greeting
Sich Kennenlernen und Begrüßen

Hello!
Guten Tag!

Hi!
Hallo!

How are you?
Wie geht's?

I am fine, thank you.
Danke, gut!

What is your name?
Wie heißt du denn?

My name is Maria.
What is your name?
**Ich heiße Maria.
Und wie heißt du?**

My name is Susan.
Ich heiße Susanne.

What a beautiful day!
Was für ein schöner Tag!

Do you live near the park?
Wohnst du nahe beim Park?

Yes, I live across the street.
Ja, ich wohne gleich über der Straße.

Where do you live?
Wo wohnst denn du?

I live on Main Street.
Ich wohne in der Hauptstraße.

Do you know what time it is?
Weißt du, wie spät es ist?

It is three o'clock.
Es ist drei Uhr.

Oh, I have to go now.
Ach, ich muss jetzt gehen.

It was nice to meet you.
Es war nett, dich zu treffen.

Good-bye!
Auf Wiedersehen!

See you soon!
Bis bald!

123

Word List

A

Abendessen (das), dinner, 31
Abenteuer (das), adventure, 7
aber, but, 20
abschließen (...zu...), to lock, 60
Abteilung (die) (...abteilung), department, 31
acht, eight, 68
achtzehn, eighteen, 68
achtzig, eighty, 68
Affe (der), monkey, 10
alle, all, 8
alles, everything, 35
Alligator (der), alligator, 10
alt, old, 71
am besten, best, 16
Ameise (die), ant, 52
andere, other, 73
anders, different, 31
anfangen, to begin, 15
anfangen, to start, 98
Angst haben, to be afraid, 7
anhalten, to stop, 98
anrufen (...zu...), to call, 21
ansehen (...zu...), to look, 60
antworten, to answer, 8
Anzug (der), suit, 99
Apfel (der), apple, 9
Apfelsine (die), orange, 72
April (der), April, 9
Arbeit (die), job, 54
Arbeit (die), work, 117
arbeiten, to work, 117
Arbeitszimmer (das), office, 86
Arm (der), arm, 76
arm, poor, 81
Art (die), kind, 55
Arzt (der), doctor, 32
Ast (der), branch, 18
auch, too, 106
auf, on, 71
auf, upon, 111
Auf Wiedersehen, good-bye, 42
Aufführung (die), show, 93
aufhören, to quit, 83
aufwachen, to wake up, 113
Auge (das), eye, 76
August (der), August, 12
Auto (das), car, 108
autsch, ouch, 73

B

Baby (das), baby, 13
Bäckerei (die), bakery, 13
Backofen (der), oven, 73
Bad (das), bath, 14
Badezimmer (das), bathroom, 86
bald, soon, 96
Ball (der), ball, 13
Ballon (der), balloon, 13
Banane (die), banana, 13
Bär (der), bear, 10
Baseball (der), baseball, 44
Basketball (der), basketball, 44
Bauch (der), stomach, 76
bauen, to build, 19
Baum (der), tree, 107
bedeuten, to mean, 62
beenden, to end, 35
Beere (die), berry, 16
behalten, to keep, 55
bei, by, 20
beige, tan, 68
begeistert, excited, 35
Bein (das), leg, 76
bekommen, to get, 41
bellen, to bark, 14
benutzen, to use, 111
Berg (der), mountain, 65
berühren, to touch, 76
beschäftigt, busy, 20
Besen (der), broom, 19
besitzen, to own, 73
besonderes, special, 97
besorgt, worried, 117
besser, better, 16
besuchen, to visit, 112
Bett (das), bed, 15
Bettdecke (die), quilt, 83
bevor, before, 15
Biene (die), bee, 52
Bild (das), picture, 79
binden, to tie, 105
bis, until, 111
bitte, please, 80
blasen, to blow, 17
Blatt (das), leaf, 57
blau, blue, 68
bleiben, to stay, 98
Bleistift (der), pencil, 75
Blitz (der), lightning, 59
Blume (die), flower, 39

Bluse (die), blouse, 24
Bohnen (die), beans, 15
Bonbon (der), candy, 21
Boot (das), boat, 108
brauchen, to need, 66
braun, brown, 68
Brief (der), letter, 58
Briefkasten (der), mailbox, 61
Briefmarke (die), stamp, 97
Briefträger (der), mail carrier, 61
Brille (die), glasses, 42
bringen, to bring, 19
Brot (das), bread, 18
Brücke (die), bridge, 19
Bruder (der), brother, 19
Buch (das), book, 17
Bücherei (die), library, 58
Buchhandlung (die), bookstore, 17
Buntstift (der), crayon, 29
Bürgermeister (der), mayor, 62
Bürgersteig (der), sidewalk, 93
Bürste (die), brush, 19
Bus (der), bus, 108
Busch (der), bush, 20
Butter (die), butter, 20
Butterbrot (das), sandwich, 90

C

Clown (der), clown, 28
Computer (der), computer, 28

D

Dach (das), roof, 88
Dachboden (der), attic, 86
danken, to thank, 102
dann, then, 103
das, that, 102
Daumen (der), thumb, 76
Decke (die), blanket, 17
dein, your, 118
Dekorationen (die), decorations, 30
Delphin (der), dolphin, 32
denken, to think, 104
der, die, das, des, dem, den, the, 103
Dezember (der), December, 30

dick, fat, 36
die, those, 104
Dienstag (der), Tuesday, 110
dies, this, 104
diese, these, 103
Ding (das), thing, 103
Dinosaurier (der), dinosaur, 31
Donner (der), thunder, 104
Donnerstag (der), Thursday, 105
Dorf (das), village, 112
dort, there, 103
Dose (die), can, 21
Drache (der), dragon, 33
Drachen (der), kite, 56
draußen, outdoors, 73
drehen, to turn, 110
drei, three, 68
Dreieck (das), triangle, 107
dreißig, thirty, 68
dreizehn, thirteen, 68
drinnen, inside, 51
drücken, to push, 82
du, you, 118
dunkel, dark, 30
dünn, thin, 103
durch, through, 104
durstig, thirsty, 104

E

echt, real, 85
Ehefrau (die), wife, 116
Ehemann (der), husband, 50
Ei (das), egg, 34
Eichhörnchen (das), squirrel, 97
ein, a/an, 7
eines Tages, someday, 96
einhämmern (...zu...), to pound, 81
einige, some, 96
einkaufen, to shop, 92
einmal, once, 72
eins, one, 68
Eis (das), ice, 51
Eiscreme (die), ice cream, 51
Elefant (der), elephant, 10
elf, eleven, 68
Eltern (die), parents, 74
Ente (die), duck, 10
entlang, along, 8
Entscheidung (die), decision, 30

er, he, 47
Erbse (die), pea, 75
Erdbeere (die), strawberry, 99
Erde (die), ground, 46
Esel (der), donkey, 32
Essen (das), food, 39
Esszimmer (das), dining room, 86
etwas, something, 96
Eule (die), owl, 73

F

Fabrik (die), factory, 36
Fahne (die), flag, 38
fahren, to drive, 33
Fahrrad (das), bicycle, 108
fallen lassen, to drop, 33
falsch, wrong, 117
Familie (die), family, 36
fangen, to catch, 23
Farbe (die), paint, 74
fast, almost, 8
faul, lazy, 57
Fäustlinge (die), mittens, 24
Februar (der), February, 37
Feder (die), feather, 37
feiern, to celebrate, 23
Felsen (der), rock, 88
Fenster (das), window, 116
Fernsehen (das), television, 102
fertig, ready, 84
Feuer (das), fire, 37
Feuerwehrgebäude (das), firehouse, 38
Feuerwehrmann (der), firefighter, 38
Film (der), movie, 65
finden, to find, 37
Finger (der), finger, 76
Fisch (der), fish, 10
Flasche (die), bottle, 18
Fledermaus (die), bat, 14
Fleisch (das), meat, 62
Fliege (die), fly, 52
fliegen, to fly, 39
Floh (der), flea, 52
Flöte (die), flute, 39
Flughafen (der), airport, 8
Flugzeug (das), airplane, 108
Flur (der), hall, 86
Fluss (der), river, 88
flüstern, to whisper, 115
fortgehen, to leave, 58
Foto (das), photograph, 78
Frage (die), question, 83
fragen, to ask, 12
Frau (die), woman, 117
Frau, Mrs., 65

Freitag (der), Friday, 40
(fr)essen, to eat, 34
Freund (der), friend, 40
freundlich, kind, 55
Friseur (der), barber, 14
fröhlich, happy, 47
Frosch (der), frog, 10
früh, early, 34
Frühling (der), spring, 97
Frühstück (das), breakfast, 18
Fuchs (der), fox, 10
fühlen, to feel, 37
Füller (der), pen, 75
fünf, five, 68
fünfzehn, fifteen, 68
fünfzig, fifty, 68
für, for, 39
Fuß (der), foot, 76
Fußball (der), soccer, 44
Fußboden (der), floor, 38

G

Gabel (die), fork, 39
Gähnen (das), yawn, 118
Gans (die), goose, 42
ganz, whole, 116
Garage (die), garage, 86
Garten (der), garden, 41
Garten (der), yard, 118
geben, to give, 41
Geburtstag (der), birthday, 17
Gefahr (die), danger, 30
gegenüber, across, 7
Geheimnis (das), secret, 91
gehen, to go, 42
Geige (die), violin, 112
gelb, yellow, 68
Geld (das), money, 64
Gemüse (das), vegetable, 112
genug, enough, 35
Gerümpel (das), junk, 54
Geschäft (das), store, 98
Geschenk (das), present, 81
Geschichte (die), story, 99
Geschirr (das), dish, 32
Gesicht (das), face, 76
gestern, yesterday, 118
gesund, well, 114
Giraffe (die), giraffe, 10
Gitarre (die), guitar, 46
Glas (das), glass, 42
Glas (das), jar, 54
glauben, to believe, 16
gleich, same, 90
Glocke (die), bell, 16
Glühwürmchen (das), firefly, 52
Golf (das), golf, 44
Gorilla (der), gorilla, 43

Gottesanbeterin (die), mantis, 52
graben, to dig, 31
Gras (das), grass, 43
grau, gray, 68
greifen, to grab, 43
Grille (die), cricket, 52
groß, big, 16
groß, tall, 101
Großmutter (die), grandma, 43
Großmutter (die), grandmother, 43
Großvater (der), grandfather, 43
Großvater (der), grandpa, 43
grün, green, 68
Gruppe (die), group, 46
Gürtel (der), belt, 24
Gürteltier (das), armadillo, 9
gut, good, 42
gut, well, 114
Guten Tag, hello, 48

H

Haar (das), hair, 76
haben, to have, 47
Hahn (der), rooster, 10
Hai (der), shark, 92
halb, half, 47
hallo, hi, 48
Hals (der), neck, 76
halten, to hold, 49
Hammer (der), hammer, 47
Hand, hand, 76
Handschuhe (die), gloves, 24
Handtasche (die), purse, 82
Handtuch (das), towel, 106
Hängematte (die), hammock, 47
Harfe (die), harp, 47
hart, hard, 47
hässlich, ugly, 111
Haus (das), house, 50
Haustier (das), pet, 78
heiß, hot, 49
Hemd (das), shirt, 24
Herbst (der), fall, 36
hereinlegen (...zu...), to trick, 107
Herr, Mr., 65
Herz (das), heart, 48
Heuschrecke (die), grasshopper, 52
heute, today, 105
heute Abend, tonight, 106
hier, here, 48
Hilfe (die), help, 48
Himmel (der), sky, 94
hinaus, out, 73

hinfallen, to fall, 36
hinfallen (...zu...), to trip, 107
hinter, behind, 16
hoch, high, 48
höflich, polite, 80
Höhle (die), cave, 23
Holzterrasse (die), deck, 86
hören, to hear, 76
hören (...hören), to listen, 59
Horn (das), horn, 49
Hosen (die), pants, 24
Hotel (das), hotel, 49
Hubbel (der), bump, 19
hübsch, pretty, 81
Hubschrauber (der), helicopter, 108
Hügel (der), hill, 48
Huhn (das), chicken, 10
Hund (der), dog, 32
Hündchen (das), puppy, 82
hundert, hundred, 68
hungrig, hungry, 50
hüpfen, to hop, 49
hurra, hooray, 49
Hut (der), hat, 24

I

ich, I, 51
Idee (die), idea, 51
ihnen, them, 103
ihr, her, 48
ihr, their, 103
in, in, 51
in, into, 51
Insel (die), island, 51

J

ja, yes, 118
Jacke (die), jacket, 24
Jaguar (der), jaguar, 10
Jahr (das), year, 118
Januar (der), January, 54
jede, each, 34
jeder, everyone, 35
jedes, every, 35
jemand, someone, 96
jetzt, now, 70
Juli (der), July, 54
Junge (der), boy, 18
Juni (der), June, 54

K

Käfer (der), beetle, 52
Käfer (der), bug, 19
Käfig (der), cage, 21
kalt, cold, 28
Kamel (das), camel, 21

Kamera (die), camera, 21
Kamm (der), comb, 28
kämmen, to comb, 28
Känguru (das), kangaroo, 10
Kaninchen (das), rabbit, 10
Kapelle (die), band, 13
Karotte (die), carrot, 22
Karte (die), card, 22
Kartoffel (die), potato, 81
Käse (der), cheese, 23
Kastagnetten (die), castanets, 22
Kätzchen (das), kitten, 56
Katze (die), cat, 22
kaufen, to buy, 20
Kegeln (das), bowling, 44
Keller (der), basement, 86
kennenlernen (...zu...), to meet, 63
Kerze (die), candle, 21
Kette (die), necklace, 66
Kind (das), child, 26
Kirsche (die), cherry, 26
Kiste (die), box, 18
Klasse (die), class, 26
Klassenzimmer (das), classroom, 27
klatschen, to clap, 26
Klavier (das), piano, 78
klebrig, sticky, 98
Kleid (das), dress, 24
klein, little, 59
klein, short, 93
klein, small, 95
klettern, to climb, 27
klopfen, to knock, 56
Knie (das), knee, 76
Knopf (der), button, 20
kochen, to cook, 28
Koffer (der), suitcase, 99
komisch, funny, 40
kommen, to come, 28
König (der), king, 55
Königin (die), queen, 83
Kopf (der), head, 76
Kopfkissen (das), pillow, 79
Korb (der), basket, 14
krank, sick, 93
Krankenhaus (das), hospital, 49
Krankenschwester (die), nurse, 70
Krawatte (die), tie, 24
Kreide (die), chalk, 23
Kreis (der), circle, 26
Kricket (das), cricket, 44
Küche (die), kitchen, 86
Kuchen (der), cake, 21
Kuchen (der), pie, 79

Kuh (die), cow, 10
Kühlschrank, (der) refrigerator, 85
Kunst (die), art, 9
Kuss (der), kiss, 55

L

Lächeln (das), smile, 95
lachen, to laugh, 57
Lama (das), llama, 10
Lampe (die), lamp, 57
Landkarte (die), map, 61
Landschaft (die), country, 29
lang, long, 60
langsam, slow, 95
Lärm (der), noise, 67
lassen, to let, 58
Lastwagen (der), truck, 108
Laufen (das), running, 44
laufen, to run, 89
laufen, to walk, 113
laut, loud, 60
laut, noisy, 67
läuten, to ring, 88
Leben (das), life, 58
leben, to live, 59
Lebensmittel (die), groceries, 46
lecken, to lick, 58
Leckerbissen (der), treat, 107
leer, empty, 34
Lehrerin (die), teacher, 101
Leid tun, to be sorry, 97
Leiter (die), ladder, 57
Leopard (der), leopard, 58
lesen, to read, 84
Leute (die), people, 78
Licht (das), light, 59
Liebe (die), love, 60
lieben, to love, 60
liebstes, favorite, 37
Lied (das), song, 96
Lieferwagen (der), van, 108
lila, purple, 68
linke, left, 58
Loch (das), hole, 49
Löffel (der), spoon, 97
Löwe (der), lion, 10
Luft (die), air, 7

M

machen, to make, 61
Mädchen (das), girl, 41
Mai (der), May, 62
Maler (der), painter, 74
Mango (die), mango, 61
Mann (der), man, 61
Mantel (der), coat, 24

Maraca (die), maraca, 62
Marmelade (die), jam, 54
März (der), March, 62
Mauer (die), wall, 113
Maus (die), mouse, 65
Medizin (die), medicine, 62
Meer (das), sea, 91
mehr, more, 64
mein, my, 65
meiste, most, 64
Messer (das), knife, 56
miau, meow, 63
mich, me, 62
Milch (die), milk, 63
Minute (die), minute, 63
mit, with, 116
mit dem Finger zeigen, to point, 80
Mittag (der), noon, 67
Mittagessen (das), lunch, 60
Mittwoch (der), Wednesday, 114
mögen, to like, 59
Monat (der), month, 64
Mond (der), moon, 64
Montag (der), Monday, 64
Morgen (der), morning, 64
morgen, tomorrow, 106
Motorrad (das), motorcycle, 108
Motte (die), moth, 52
Mücke (die), mosquito, 52
müde, tired, 105
Mund (der), mouth, 76
Musik (die), music, 65
mutig, brave, 18
Mutter (die), mother, 65
Mutti (die), mom, 64
Mütze (die), hat, 24

N

nach, after, 7
Nachbar (der), neighbor, 66
nächste, next, 67
Nacht (die), night, 67
Nagel (der), nail, 66
nahe, close, 27
Name (der), name, 66
Nase (die), nose, 76
nass, wet, 114
Nebel (der), fog, 39
neben, next, 67
nehmen (...nehmen), to take, 101
nein, no, 67
Nest (das), nest, 66
nett, nice, 67
neu, new, 66
neun, nine, 68

neunzehn, nineteen, 68
neunzig, ninety, 68
nicht, not, 70
nichts, nothing, 70
niedlich, cute, 29
niedrig, low, 60
niemals, never, 66
Nilpferd (das), hippopotamus, 10
noch, still, 98
Norden (der), north, 70
Notiz (die), note, 70
November (der), November, 70
null, zero, 68
nur, only, 72
Nuss (die), nut, 70

O

oben, top, 106
oben, up, 111
Obst (das), fruit, 40
oder, or, 72
offen, open, 72
oh, oh, 71
ohne, without, 116
Ohr (das), ear, 76
Ohrenschützer (die), earmuffs, 24
Oktober (der), October, 71
Onkel (der), uncle, 111
orange, orange, 68
Osten (der), east, 34
Ozean (der), ocean, 71

P

Panda (der), panda, 74
Papagei (der), parrot, 75
Papier (das), paper, 74
Paprikaschoten (die), peppers, 78
Parfüm (das), perfume, 78
Park (der), park, 74
Party (die), party, 75
Pfanne (die), pan, 74
Pfeffer (der), pepper, 78
Pfeife (die), whistle, 115
Pferd (das), horse, 10
Pfirsich (der), peach, 75
pflanzen, to plant, 79
Pflaster (das), bandage, 13
pflücken, to pick, 78
Pfote (die), paw, 75
Picknick (das), picnic, 78
Pinguin (der), penguin, 78
Pizza (die), pizza, 79
planen (...planen), to plan, 79

platt, flat, 38
Plätzchen (das), cookie, 28
plötzlich, suddenly, 99
Polizeirevier (das), police station, 80
Polizistin (die), police officer, 80
Post (die), mail, 61
Post (die), post office, 81
Preis (der), prize, 82
Prinz (der), prince, 81
Prinzessin (die), princess, 81
Puppe (die), doll, 32
putzen, to clean, 27
Puzzle (das), puzzle, 82

Q

Quadrat (das), square, 97
quak, quack, 83

R

Rad (das), wheel, 115
Radfahren (das), biking, 44
Radio (das), radio, 84
raten, to guess, 46
Rauch (der), smoke, 95
Raupe (die), caterpillar, 52
Rechnen (das), math, 62
rechte, right, 85
Regen (der), rain, 84
Regenbogen (der), rainbow, 84
Regenmantel (der), raincoat, 24
Regenschirm (der), umbrella, 111
Regentropfen (der), raindrop, 84
regnen, raining, 84
Reh (das), deer, 31
reiben, to rub, 89
reich, rich, 85
Reifen (der), tire, 105
Reis (der), rice, 85
Reise (die), trip, 107
Reißverschluss (der), zipper, 119
Reißverschluss zumachen (den), to zip, 119
reiten, to ride, 85
Rennen (das), race, 84
reparieren, to fix, 38
Restaurant (das), restaurant, 85
riechen, to smell, 76
riesig, huge, 50
Ring (der), ring, 88
Roboter (der), robot, 88
Rock (der), skirt, 24

Rollschuhe (die), skates, 108
Röntgenbild (das), X-ray, 118
rosa, pink, 68
Rose (die), rose, 89
rot, red, 68
Rücken (der), back, 13
rund, round, 89

S

Saft (der) (...saft), juice, 54
Säge (die), saw, 91
sagen, tell, 102
sagen, to say, 91
Salat (der), salad, 90
Salz (das), salt, 90
Samen (der), seed, 92
Samstag (der), Saturday, 90
Sand (der), sand, 90
sandig, sandy, 90
sauber, clean, 27
Schaf (das), sheep, 10
Schal (der), scarf, 24
Schale (die), bowl, 18
Schaufel (die), shovel, 93
Schere (die), scissors, 91
schicken, to send, 92
schießen, to zoom, 119
Schild (das), sign, 93
Schildkröte (die), turtle, 110
Schlafanzug (der), pajamas, 74
schlafen gehen, to sleep, 94
Schlafzimmer (das), bedroom, 86
schlagen, to hit, 49
Schläger (der), bat, 14
Schlange (die), snake, 10
schließen, to close, 86
schlimm, bad, 13
Schlittschuhlaufen (das), skating (ice), 44
Schloss (das), castle, 22
Schlüssel (der), key, 55
schmecken, to taste, 76
Schmetterling (der), butterfly, 52
schmutzig, dirty, 32
schnarchen, to snore, 95
Schnecke (die), snail, 95
Schnee (der), snow, 95
Schneeball (der), snowball, 95
schneiden, to cut, 29
schnell, fast, 36
schnell, quick, 83
Schnurrhaare (die), whiskers, 115
Schokolade (die), chocolate, 26
schon, already, 8

schön, beautiful, 15
Schoß (der), lap, 57
schrecklich, terrible, 102
schreiben, to write, 117
Schreibtisch (der), desk, 31
schreien, to shout, 93
schrubben, to scrub, 91
schüchtern, shy, 93
Schuhe (die), shoes, 24
Schüler (der), student, 99
Schwanz (der), tail, 101
schwarz, black, 68
Schwein (das), pig, 10
schwer, difficult, 31
Schwester (die), sister, 94
Schwimmen (das), swimming, 44
schwimmen, to swim, 100
sechs, six, 68
sechzehn, sixteen, 68
sechzig, sixty, 68
See (der), lake, 57
Segelboot (das), sailboat, 108
sehen, to see, 76
sehr, very, 112
Seife (die), soap, 96
Seifenblase (die), bubble, 19
sein, to be, 14
Seite (die), page, 74
Seite (die), side, 93
seltsam, strange, 99
September (der), September, 92
setzen, to place, 79
sich beeilen, to hurry, 50
sich einigen, to agree, 7
sich entscheiden, to decide, 30
sich erinnern, to remember, 85
sich freuen, to be glad, 41
sich verlaufen, to be lost, 60
sich verstecken, to hide, 48
sicher, sure, 100
sie, she, 92
sie, they, 103
sieben, seven, 68
siebzehn, seventeen, 68
siebzig, seventy, 68
singen, to sing, 94
Sitz (der), seat, 91
sitzen, to sit, 94
Skateboard (das), skateboard, 108
Skilaufen (das), skiing, 44
so, so, 96
so ... wie, as, 9
Socken (die), socks, 24
Sofa (das), sofa, 96
Sommer (der), summer, 100

Sonne (die), sun, 100
Sonnenblume (die), sunflower, 100
sonnig, sunny, 100
Sonntag (der), Sunday, 100
Sparschwein (das), bank, 14
Spaß (der), fun, 40
spät, late, 57
Spiegel (der), mirror, 63
Spiel (das), game, 41
spielen, to play, 79
Spielplatz (der), playground, 80
Spielzeug (das), toy, 107
Spielzimmer (das), playroom, 86
Spinne (die), spider, 97
Spitze (die), point, 80
sprechen, to talk, 101
springen, to jump, 54
Spur (die) (...spur), track, 107
Stadt (die), city, 26
Stadt (die), town, 107
Staub (der), dust, 33
Staubsauger (der), vacuum cleaner, 112
stecken, to put, 82
stehen, to stand, 98
Stern (der), star, 98
Stiefel (die), boots 24
still, quiet, 83
Stock (der), stick, 98
stolz, proud, 82
Strand (der), beach, 15
Straße (die), road, 88
Straße (die), street, 99
Strauß (der), ostrich, 72
streicheln, to pat, 75
streiten, to quarrel, 83
Strich (der), line, 59
Strickjacke (die), sweater, 24
Stuhl (der), chair, 23
Stunde (die), hour, 50
Sturm (der), storm, 99
Süden (der), south, 97
Suppe (die), soup, 97

T

Tag (der), day, 30
Tamburin (das), tambourine, 101
Tante (die), aunt, 12
tanzen, to dance, 30
Tasche (die), pocket, 80
Tasse (die), cup, 29
tausend, thousand, 68
Taxi (das), taxi, 108
Teich (der), pond, 80